BEST OF
LIVING DESIGN

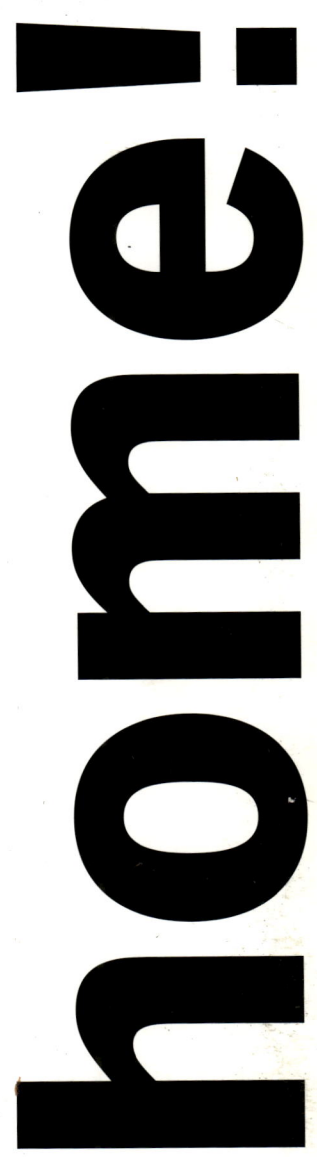

home!

Imprint

The Deutsche Bibliothek is registering this publication in the Deutsche Nationalbibliographie; detailed bibliographical information can be found on the internet at http://dnb.ddb.de

ISBN 978-3-938780-54-1
© 2008 by Verlagshaus Braun
www.verlagshaus-braun.de

1st edition 2008

Editorial staff: Annika Schulz
Translation: Stephen Roche, Hamburg
Graphic concept and layout: Michaela Prinz

BEST OF
LIVING DESIGN

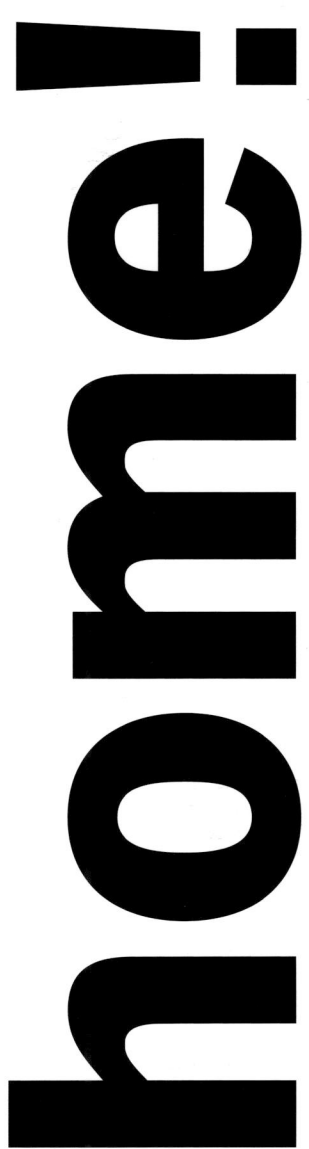

BRAUN

Preface

The idea of the living room as the focal point of private life has undergone a transformation in recent years. Having come to regard it as a mere retreat, a kind of introverted cocoon, we now increasingly recognize its importance in representing us to the outside world. Much like the parlor of old it serves as a meeting place for family and friends. This indicates a significant development; namely the crumbling of spatial boundaries. One no longer finds a closed reception room, but rather floor plans that open up and naturally incorporate functional areas such as the kitchen into the dining or living areas. Thus social trends such as the new passion for cooking together are reflected in the architectural design of the living room. The new use of form is open, unfussy and clearly structured; the debt to modernism is apparent. Not only are functional zones such as the kitchen being given an open look, but even the bathroom is being re-valuated. This formerly introverted space frequently features expansive, light-giving windows. Spaces are also being opened up vertically, with ceiling heights of over three meters no longer a rarity. Where possible, ceilings are removed altogether, creating an upper gallery.

Notwithstanding these clearly identifiable trends, this selection of about forty projects from around the world also testifies to the sheer variety of design possibilities represented by modern living spaces. Whether inspired by local materials and traditions or by modern materials, all of these projects have one thing in common: they are not concerned with creating superficial (re-)design solutions such as those featured in home makeover shows, but

are grounded in the necessary basis of all good interior design – well thought-out architecture. When it comes to designing living areas there appear to be as many desires and ideas as there are design suggestions to realize them. Designers are challenged to find creative ways to fulfill various needs – from an open view of the countryside through panoramic windows to the warmth and comfort of a crackling fire. Indeed, stoves and fireplaces are often at the heart of new apartments. A stove fulfills not only a functional but also a sculptural role alongside other monolithic design elements such as worktops, furniture or open staircases that often define the aesthetics of new living spaces. There is also great variety and freshness in the use of materials; on the one hand there is a resurgence in the use of wood, in all color tones (even a modern take on floor-to-ceiling paneling is no taboo); on the other hand, concrete is finding greater favor as an exciting and contrasting material. Although the inhabitants of these spaces are absent from all of the photos, it is clear that the designed interiors of these new living rooms invite their occupants to spend as much time as possible at home.

57 South Hill Park | London | Robert Dye Associates

Black boxes intersect and overlap, facing the landscape in different directions

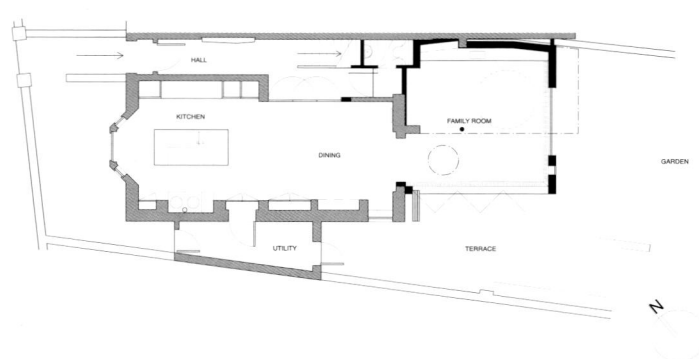

HALL

KITCHEN

DINING

FAMILY ROOM

GARDEN

UTILITY

TERRACE

N

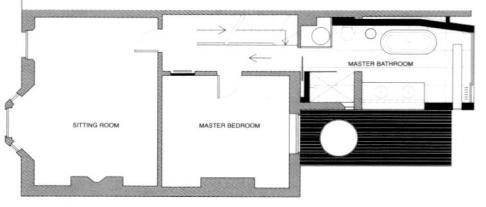

SITTING ROOM

MASTER BEDROOM

MASTER BATHROOM

N

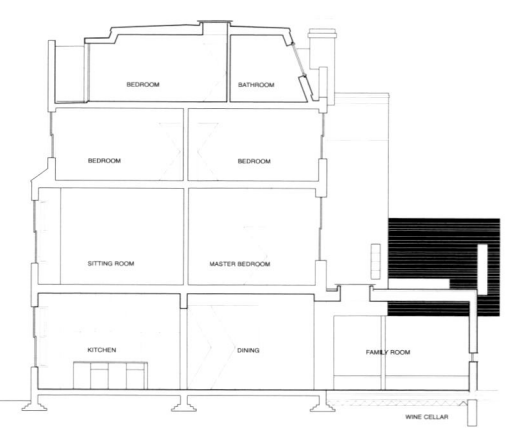

BEDROOM

BATHROOM

BEDROOM

BEDROOM

SITTING ROOM

MASTER BEDROOM

KITCHEN

DINING

FAMILY ROOM

WINE CELLAR

Actor's Home | Berlin | Design: Markus Sebastian Braun

Classic style and comfort with mobile furniture elements

Apartment in Heidelberg | Heidelberg | AAg Loebner Weber, Freie Architekten BDA

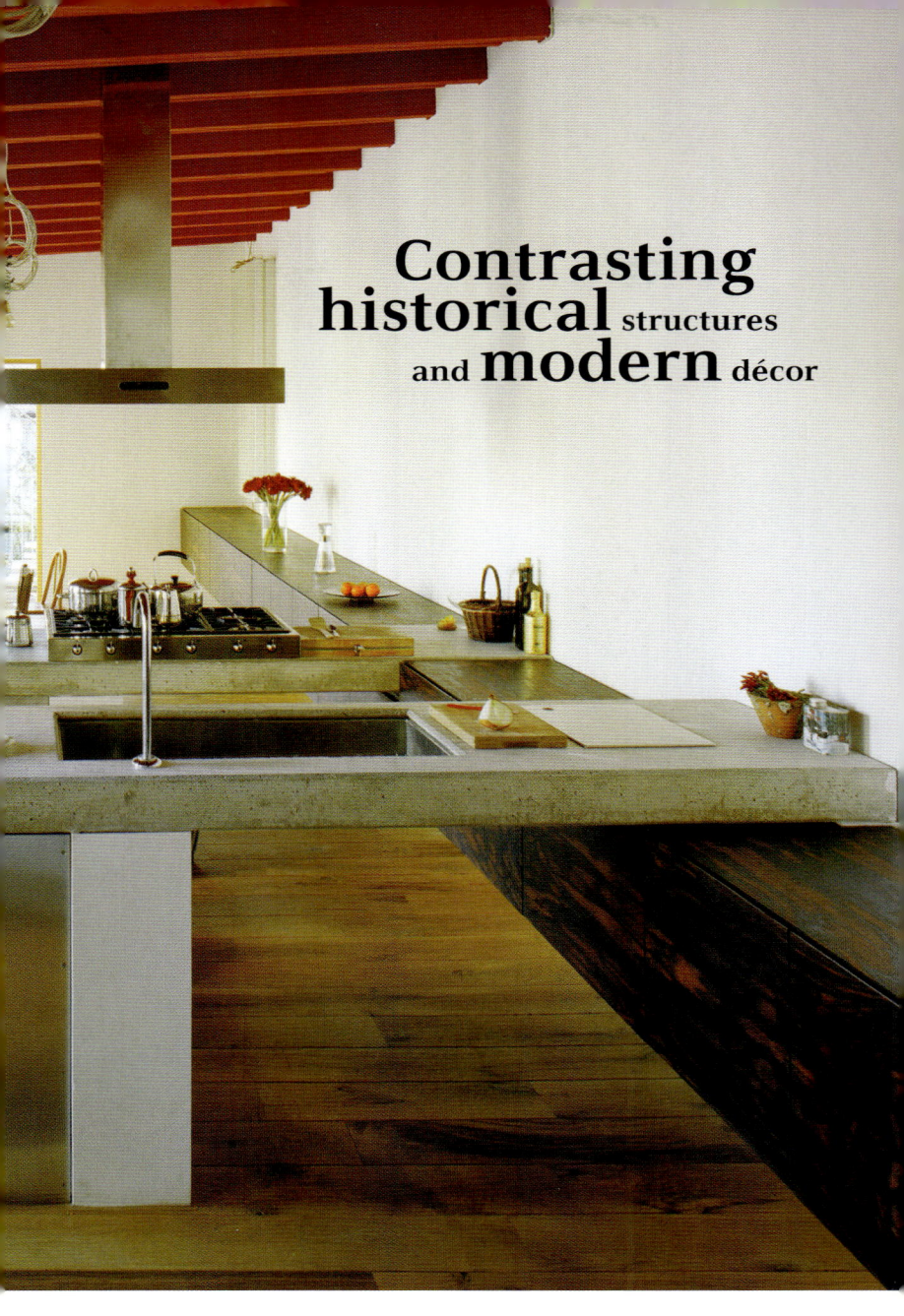

Contrasting
historical structures
and modern décor

Atelier House Meier Soglio | Soglio | Ruinelli Associati architetti

More **space** for
family living

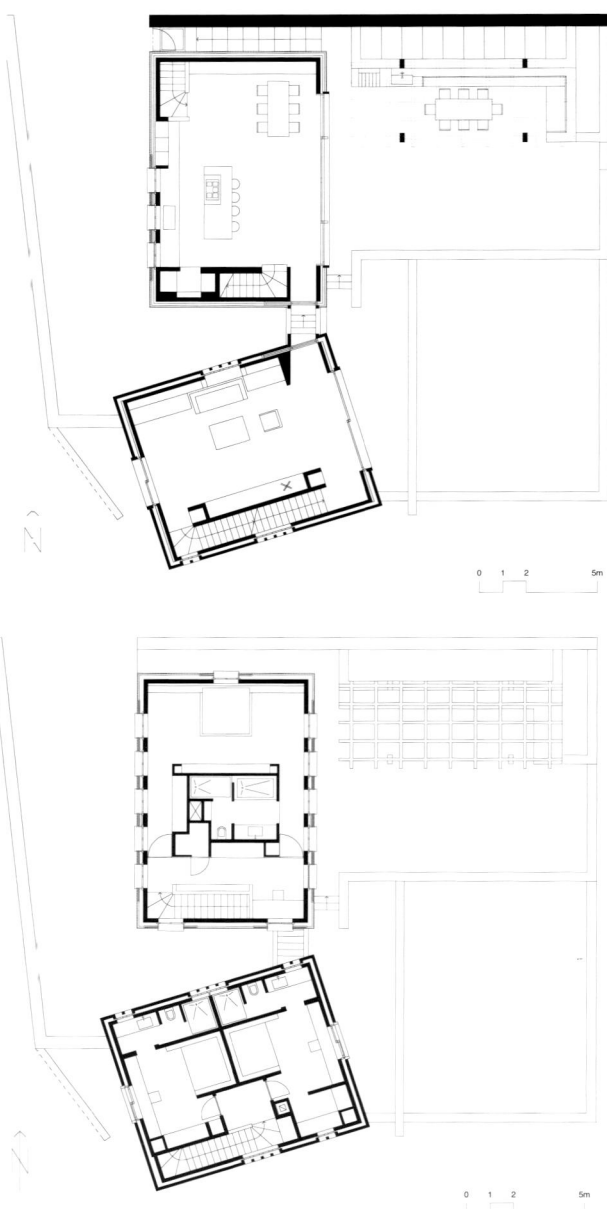

0 1 2 5m

0 1 2 5m

0 1 2   5   10m

Black Dog House | Nagano | Atelier Bow-Wow

An aesthetic and expansive interior filled with natural light

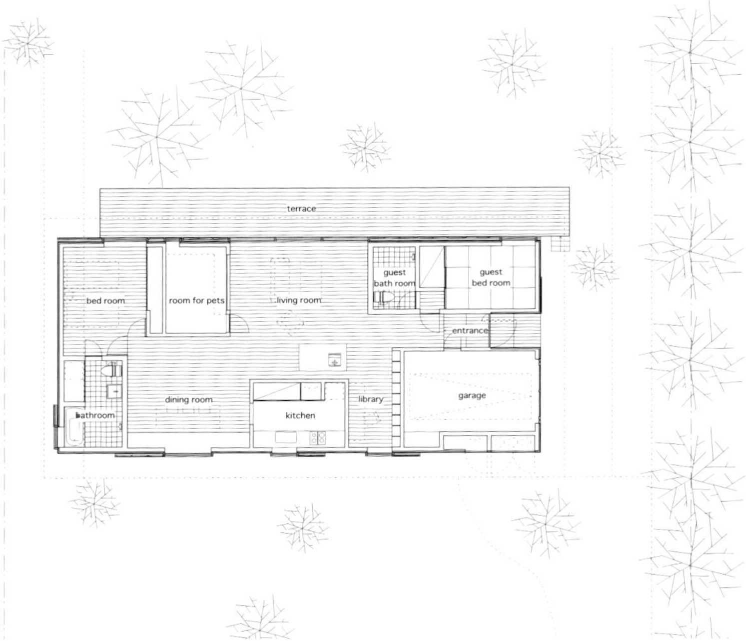

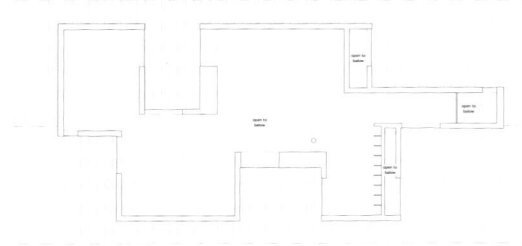

terrace
bed room
room for pets
living room
guest
bath room
guest
bed room
entrance
dining room
kitchen
library
garage
bathroom

open to
below
open to
below
open to
below
open to
below

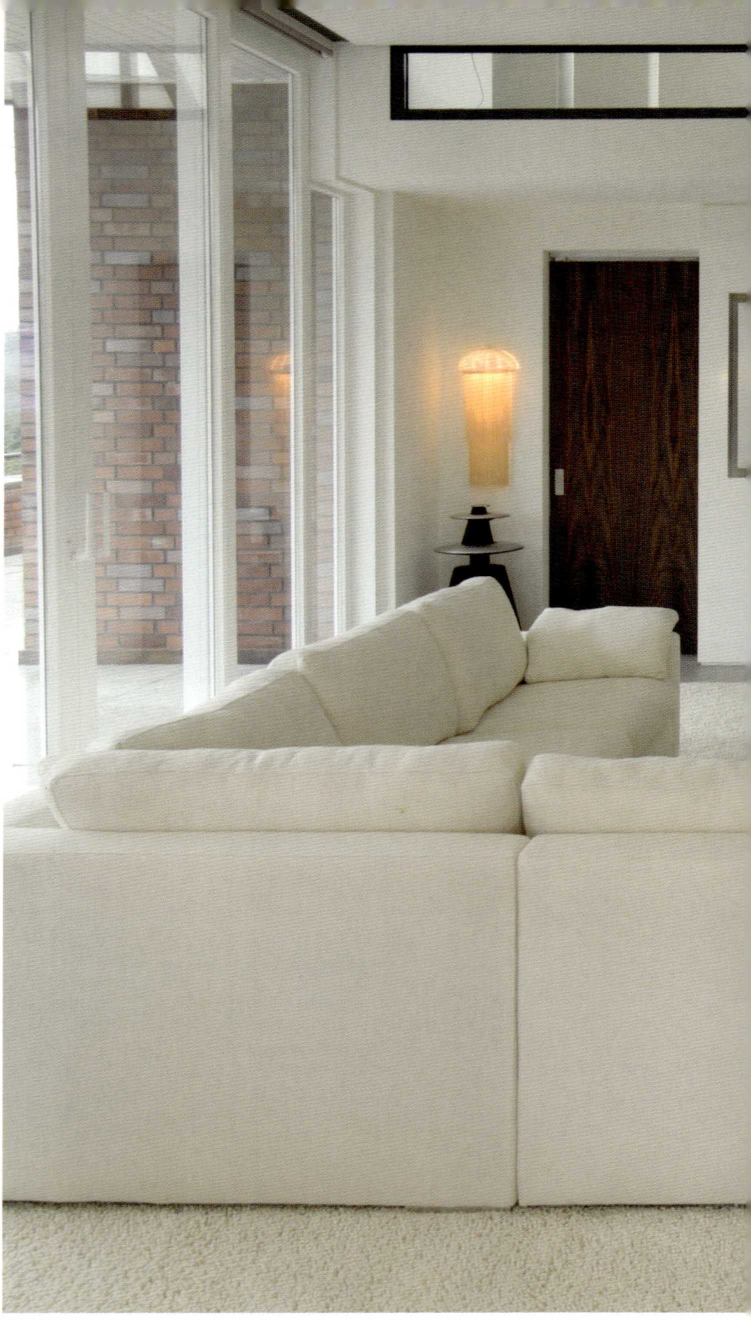

A **maximum** of **flexibility** for **individual** **living** requirements

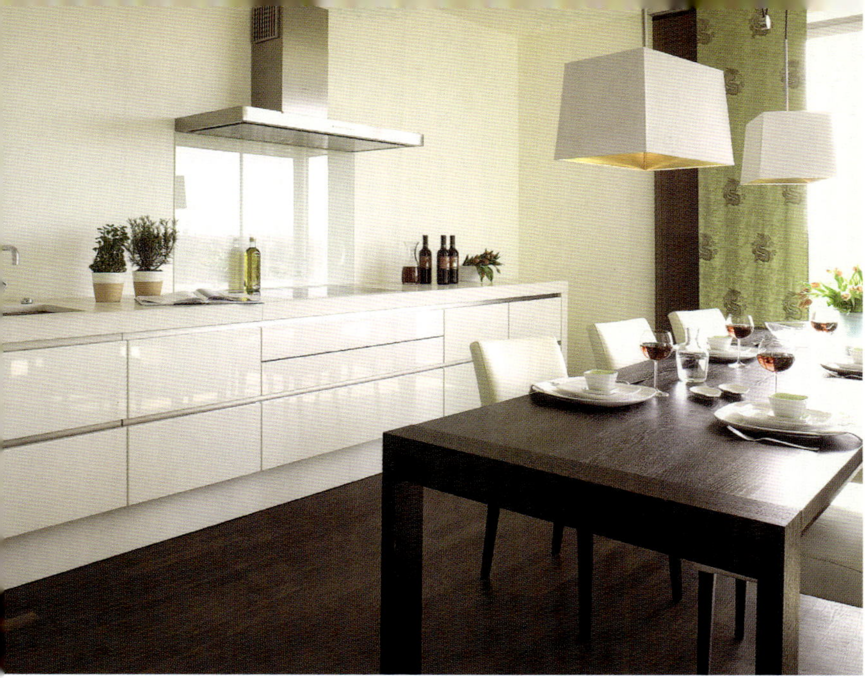

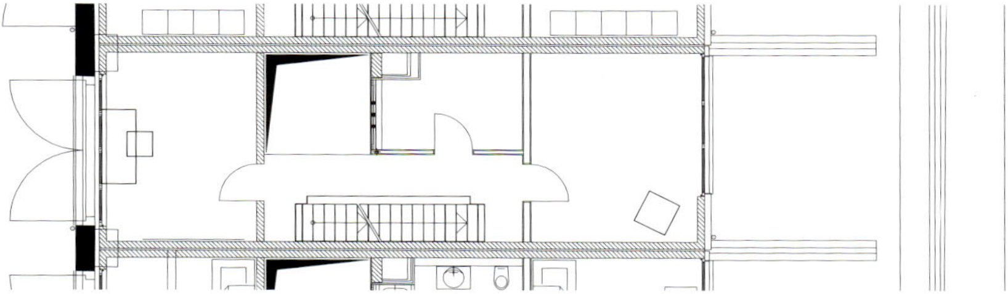

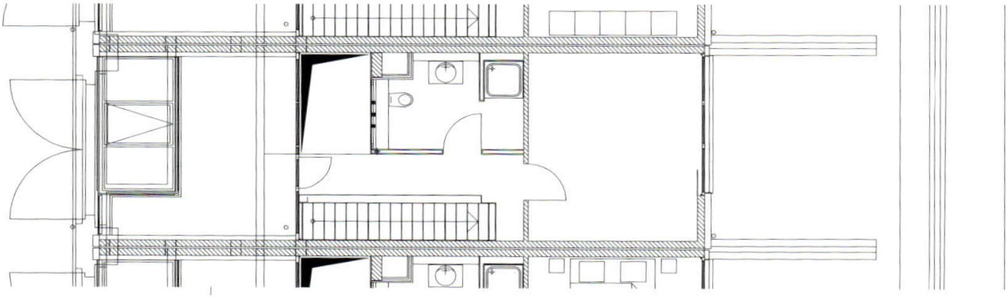

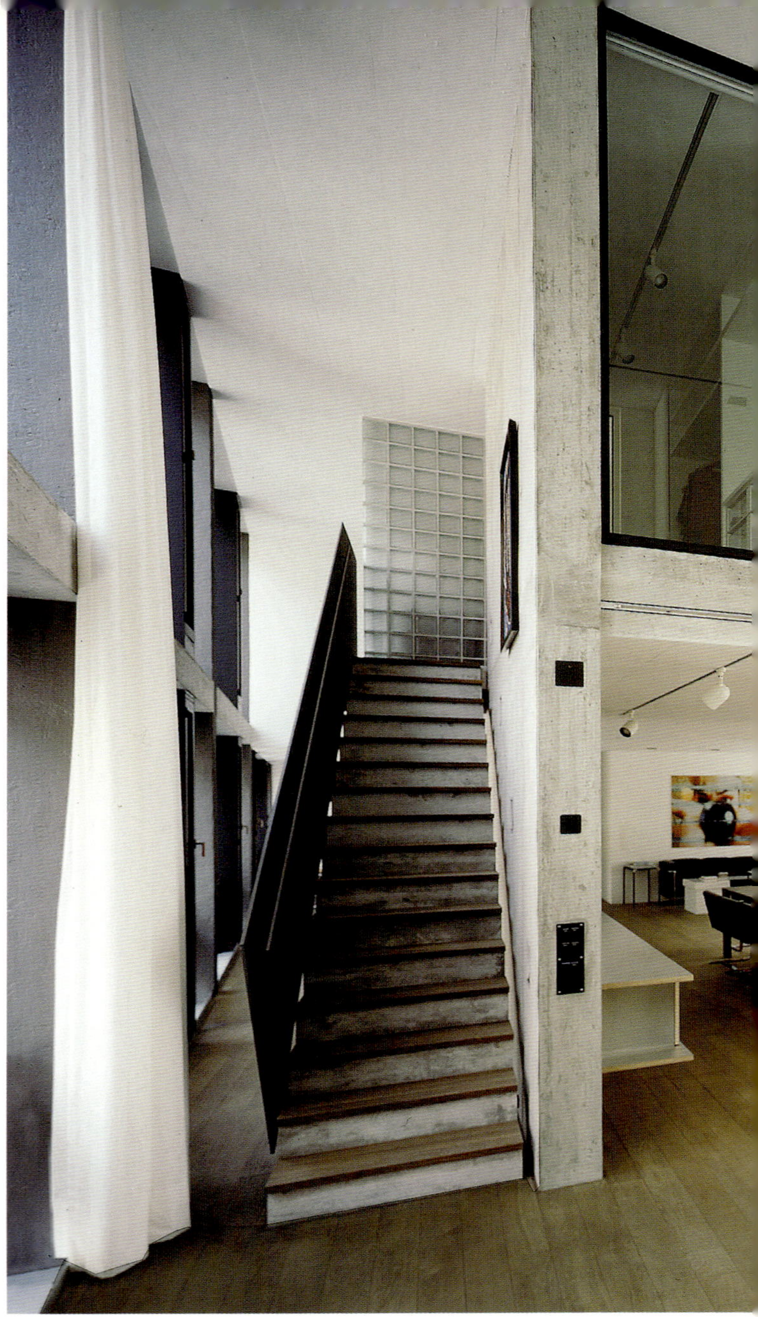

Spaces arranged in the form of a windmill

Vibrant rooms and forms that accentuate the lake view

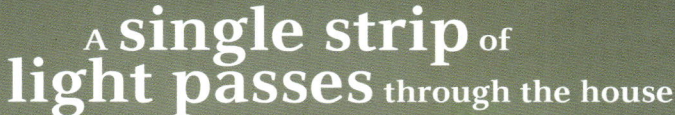

A **single strip** of **light passes** through the house

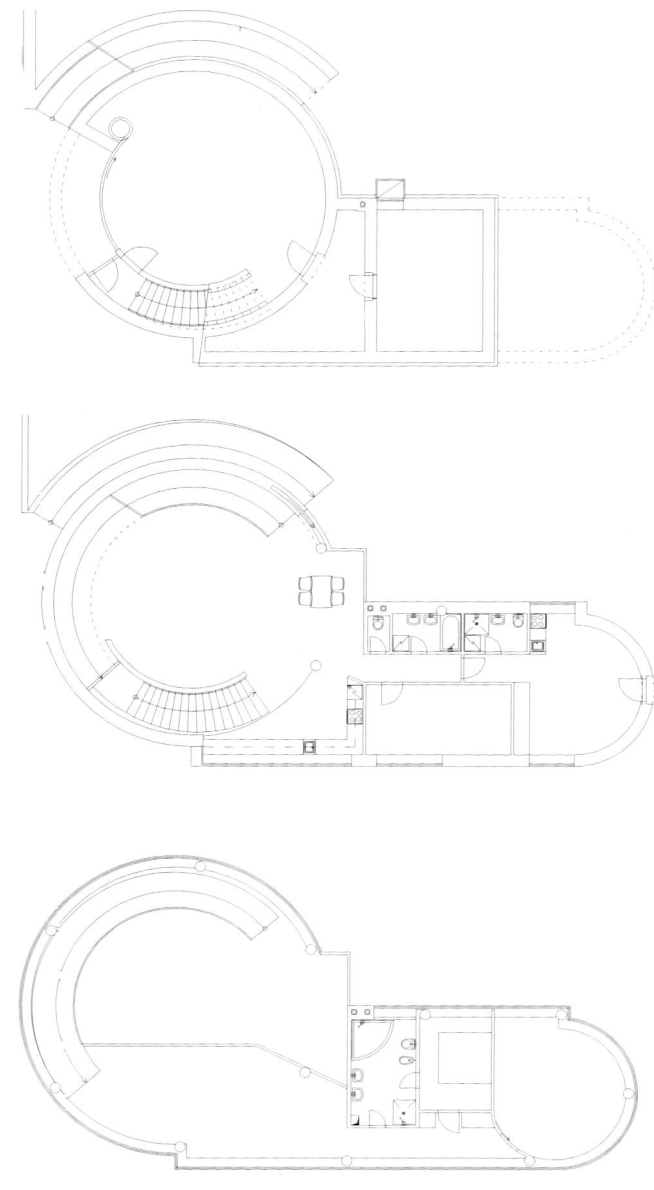

Openings cut into the walls give an impression of **fluidity** and **continuity**

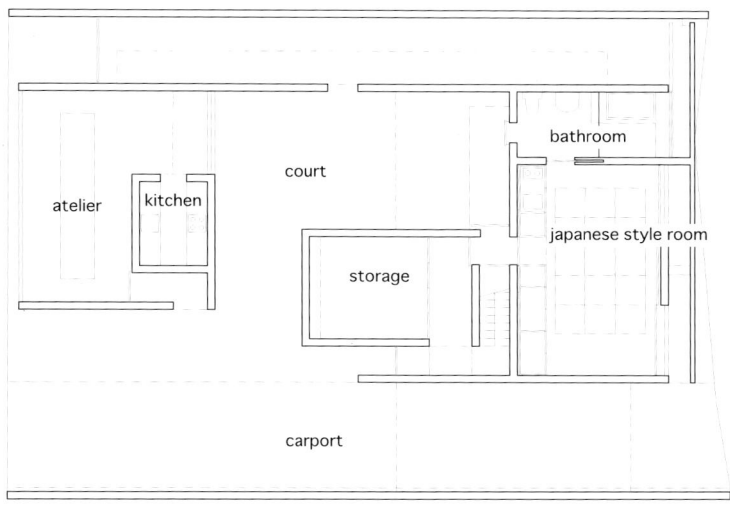

atelier

kitchen

court

bathroom

japanese style room

storage

carport

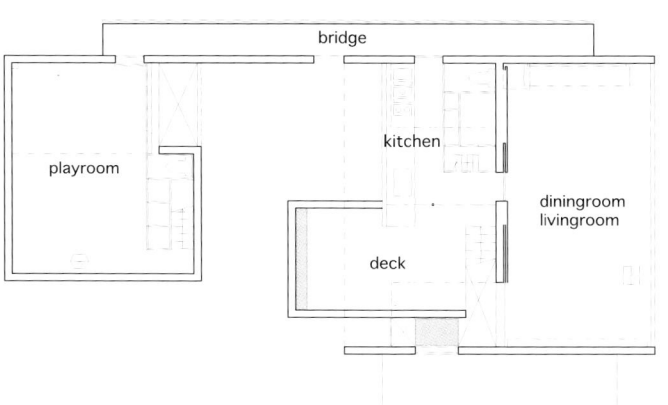

bridge

playroom

kitchen

diningroom
livingroom

deck

House Allers | Maasmechelen | Egide Meertens Architect

Clear and minimalistic shapes emphasize the design

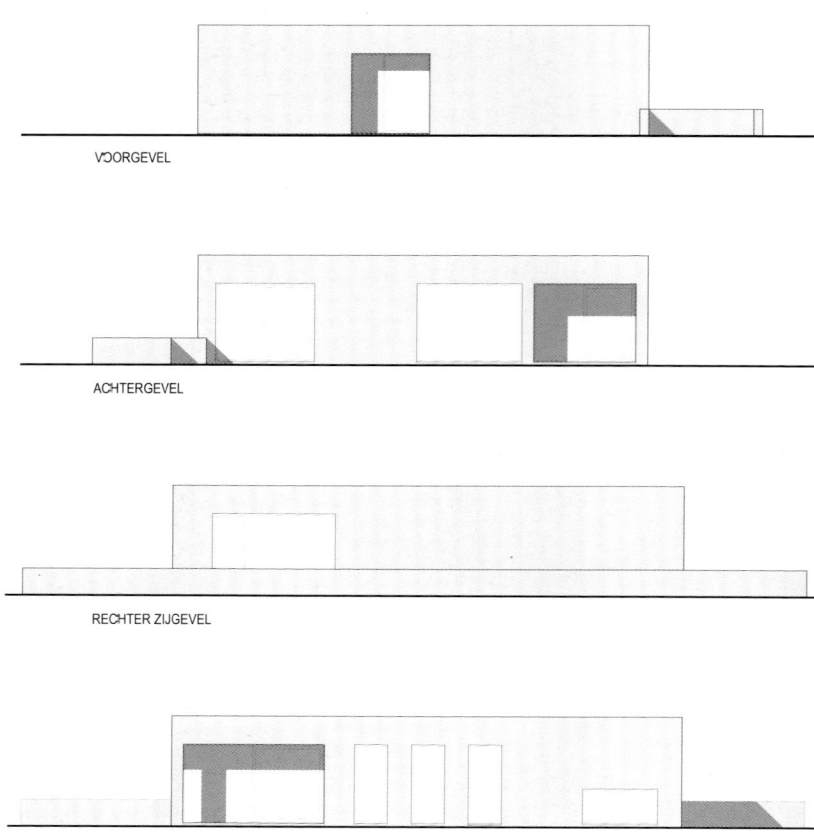

VOORGEVEL

ACHTERGEVEL

RECHTER ZIJGEVEL

LINKER ZIJGEVEL

Combining existing walls with contemporary design and clear forms

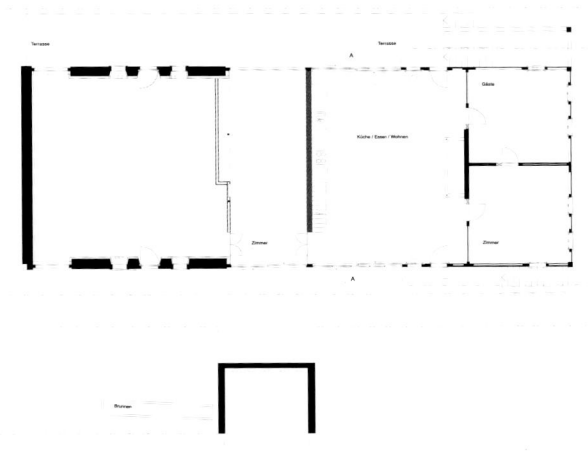

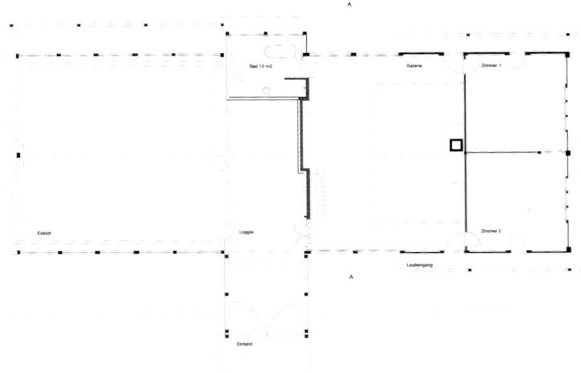

Experimental building combines spaces for family, children and work

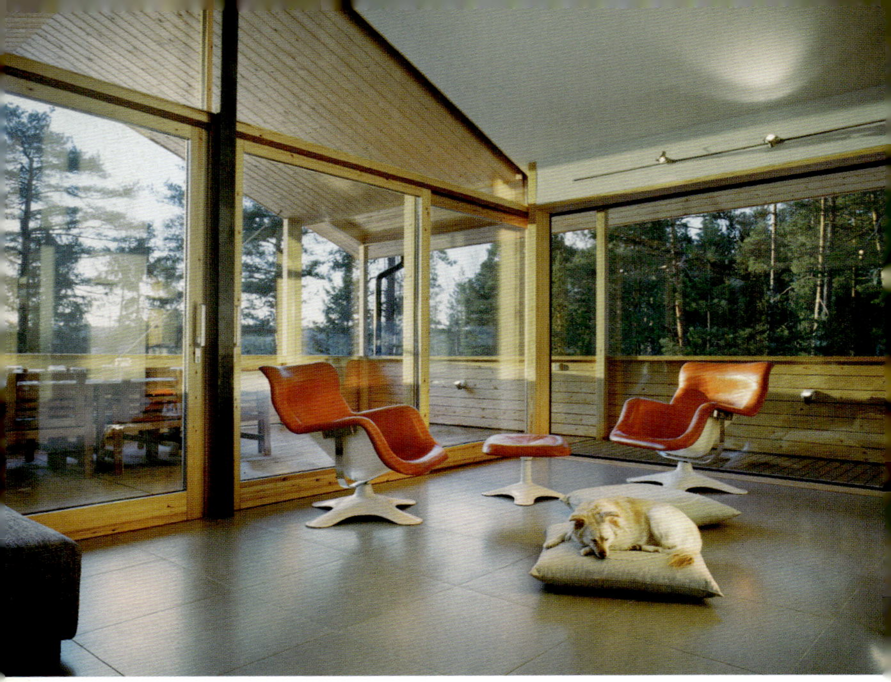

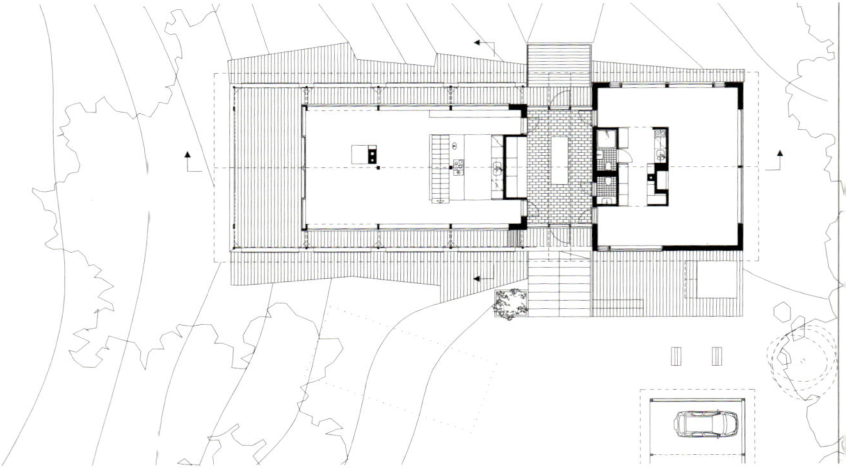

| **House Miki 1** | Stuttgart | Architekturbüro Alexander Brenner

Transparent and open spaces created by cubes and shear walls

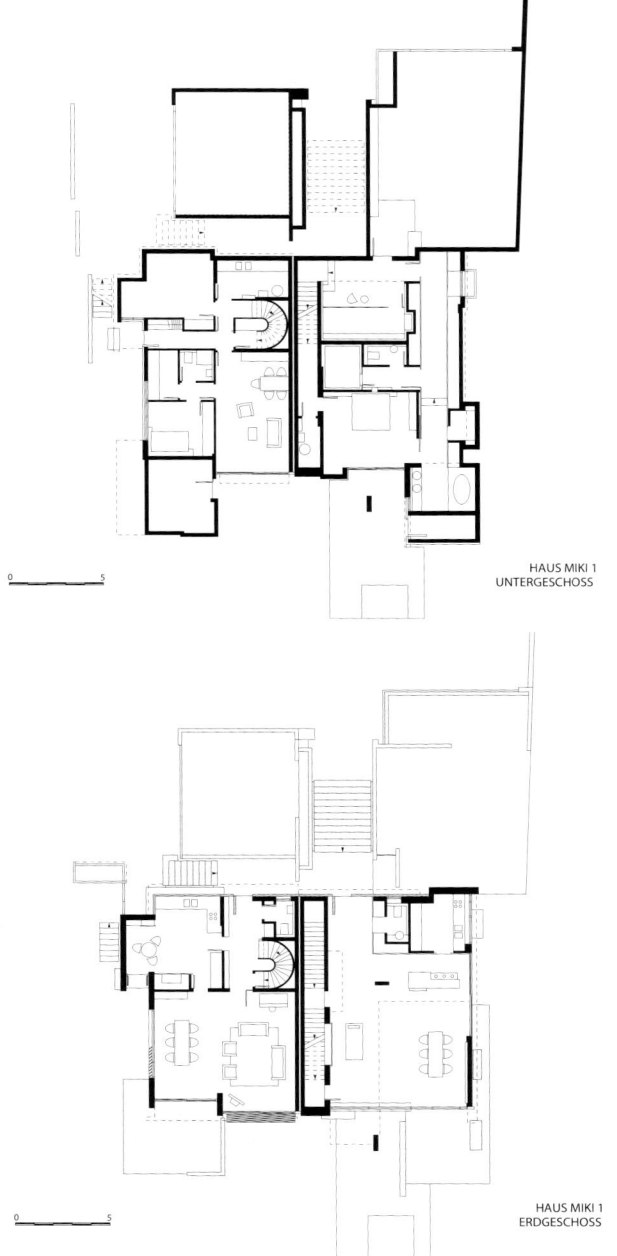

HAUS MIKI 1
UNTERGESCHOSS

0   5

HAUS MIKI 1
ERDGESCHOSS

0   5

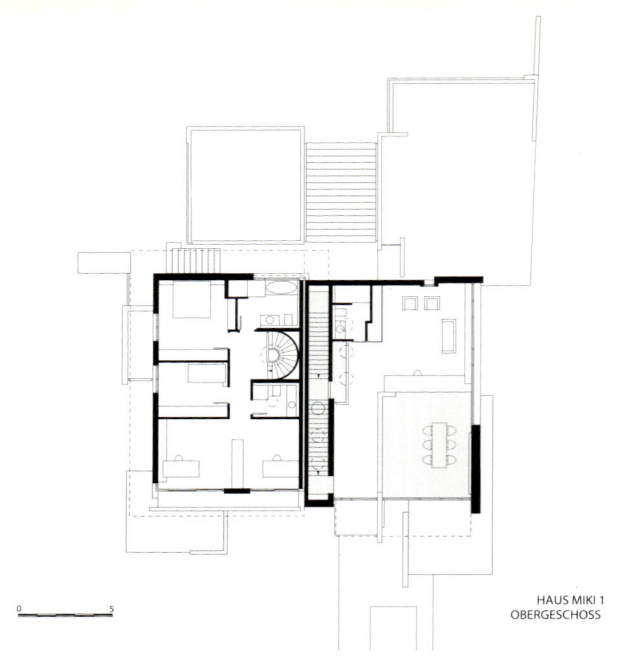

HAUS MIKI 1
OBERGESCHOSS

0 — 5

Scaled back to **natural wood beam walls** and **ceiling**

House Ribeira de Abada | Gondamor | Carlos Castanheira Architect, Castanheira & Bastei, Architects Lda.

Seeking forms
and architectural
content that defy context

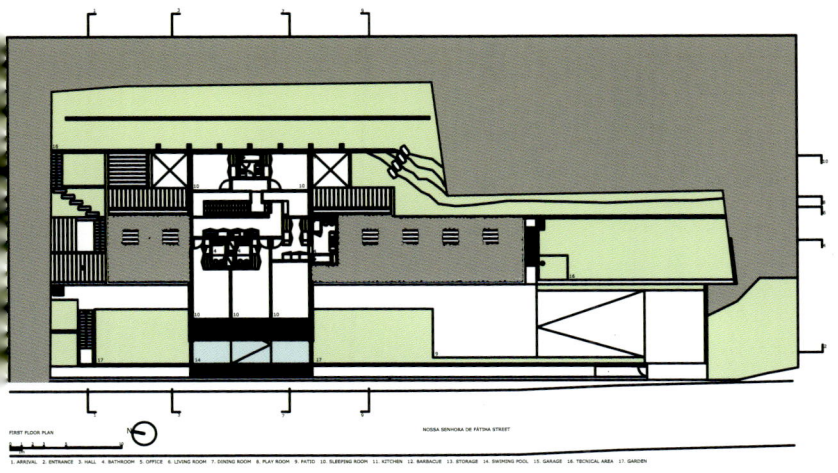

FIRST FLOOR PLAN   NOSSA SENHORA DE FÁTIMA STREET

1. ARRIVAL 2. ENTRANCE 3. HALL 4. BATHROOM 5. OFFICE 6. LIVING ROOM 7. DINING ROOM 8. PLAY ROOM 9. PATIO 10. SLEEPING ROOM 11. KITCHEN 12. BARBACUE 13. STORAGE 14. SWIMING POOL 15. GARAGE 16. TECNICAL AREA 17. GARDEN

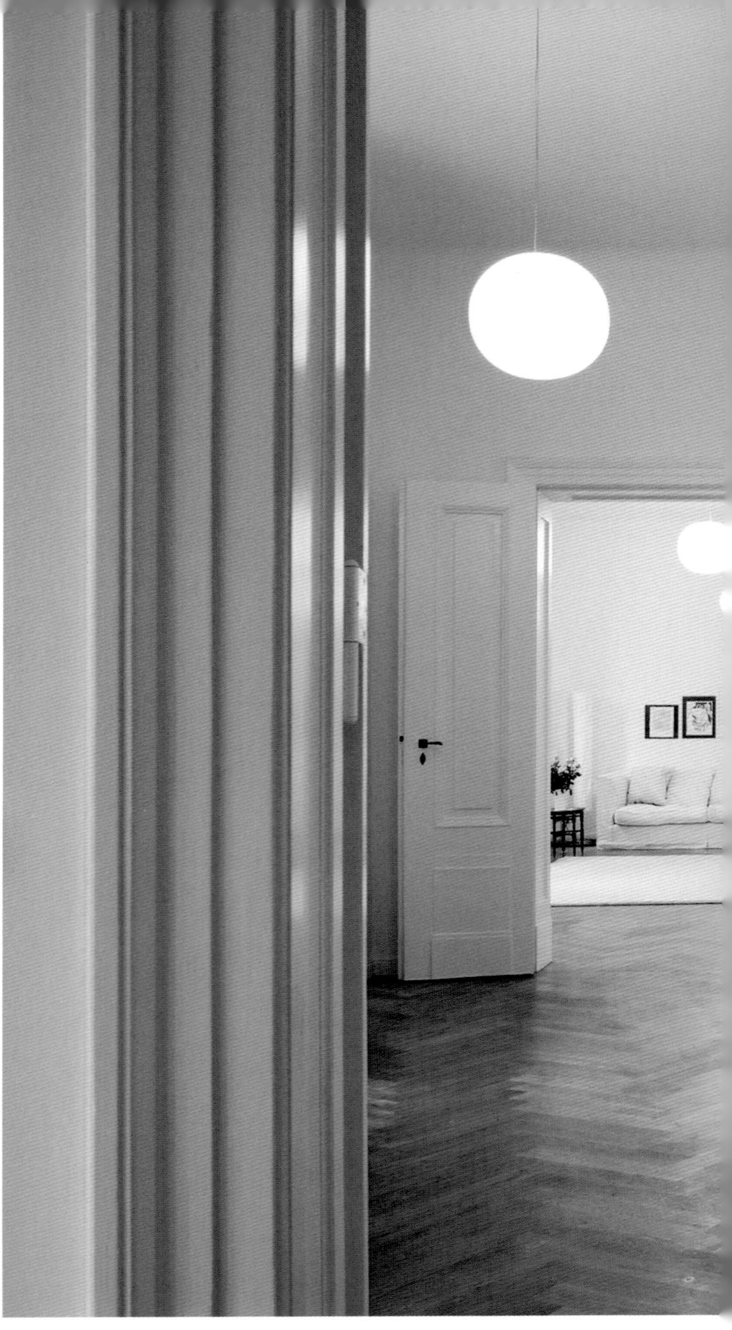

Frame motif creates boundaries and intersections

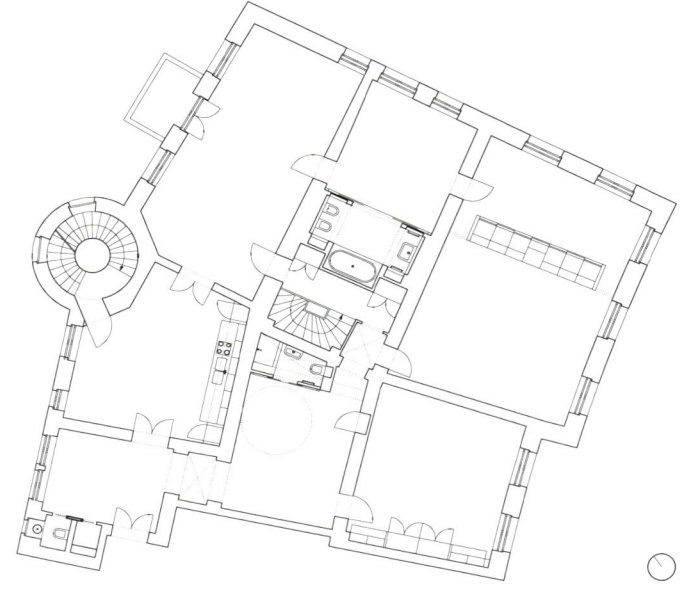

Classic-style rooms in cubic, monolithic structure

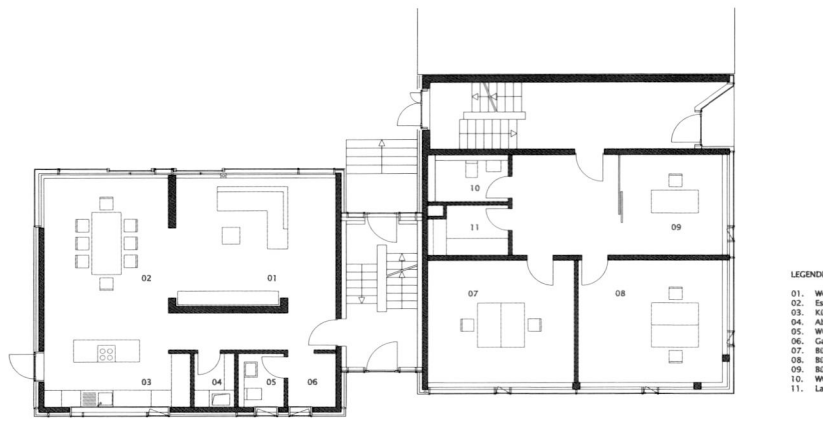

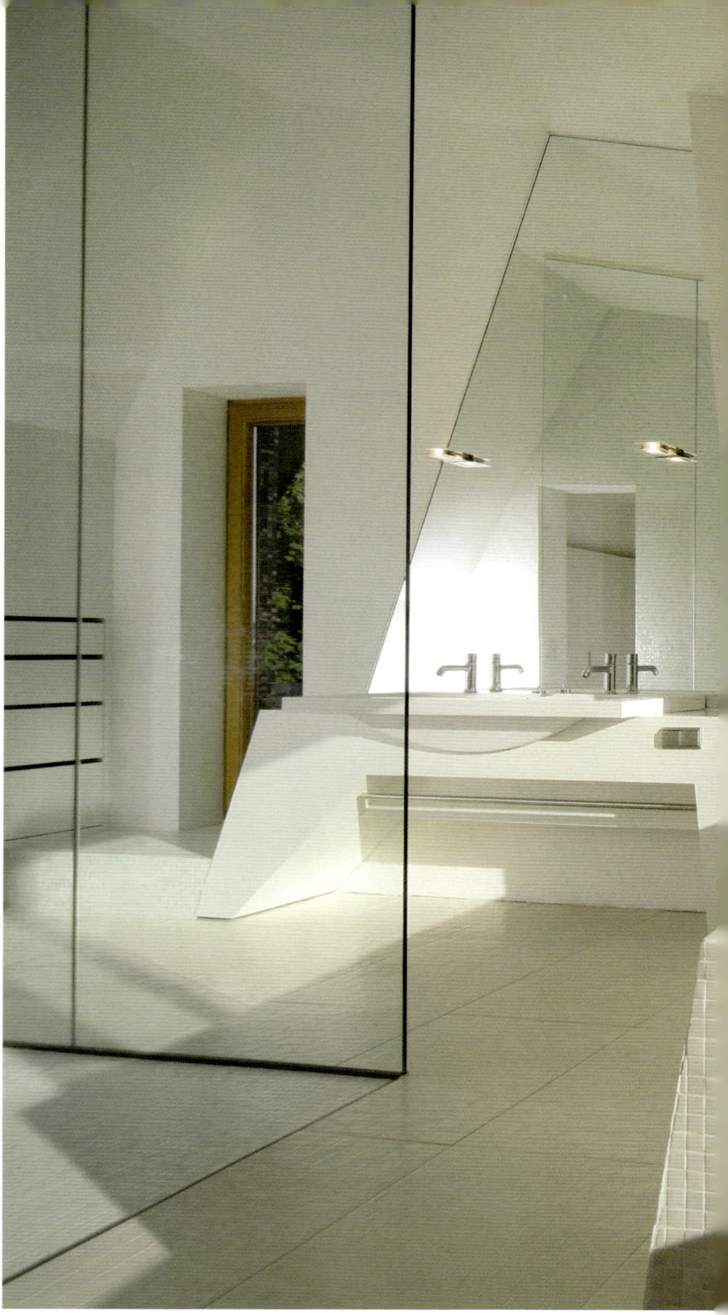

The whole structure **represents** the **glamorous architecture** of **modernity**

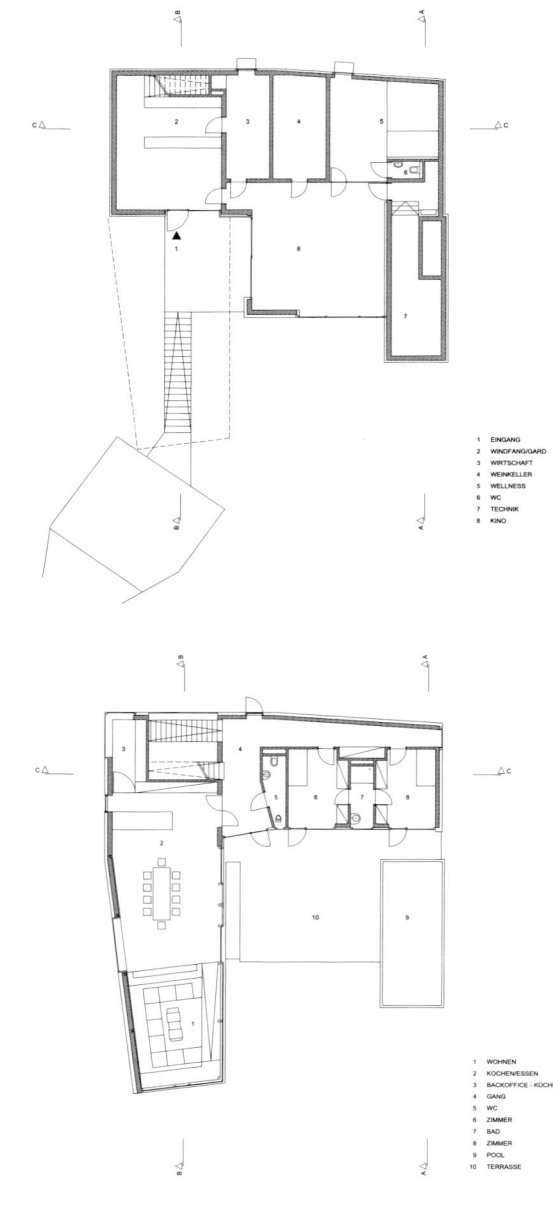

1   EINGANG
2   WINDFANG/GARD
3   WIRTSCHAFT
4   WEINKELLER
5   WELLNESS
6   WC
7   TECHNIK
8   KINO

1   WOHNEN
2   KOCHEN/ESSEN
3   BACKOFFICE - KÜCHE
4   GANG
5   WC
6   ZIMMER
7   BAD
8   ZIMMER
9   POOL
10   TERRASSE

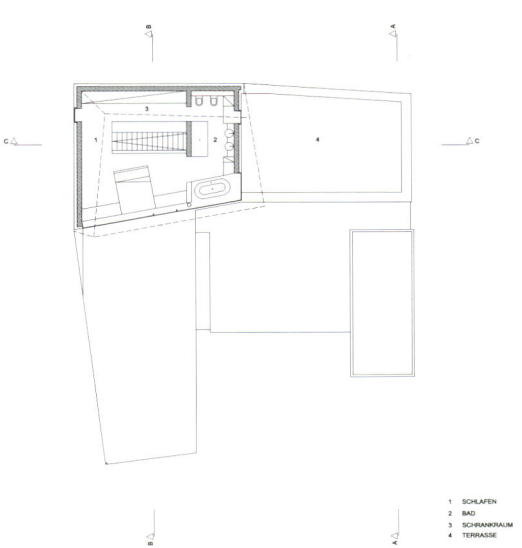

1 SCHLAFEN
2 BAD
3 SCHRANKRAUM
4 TERRASSE

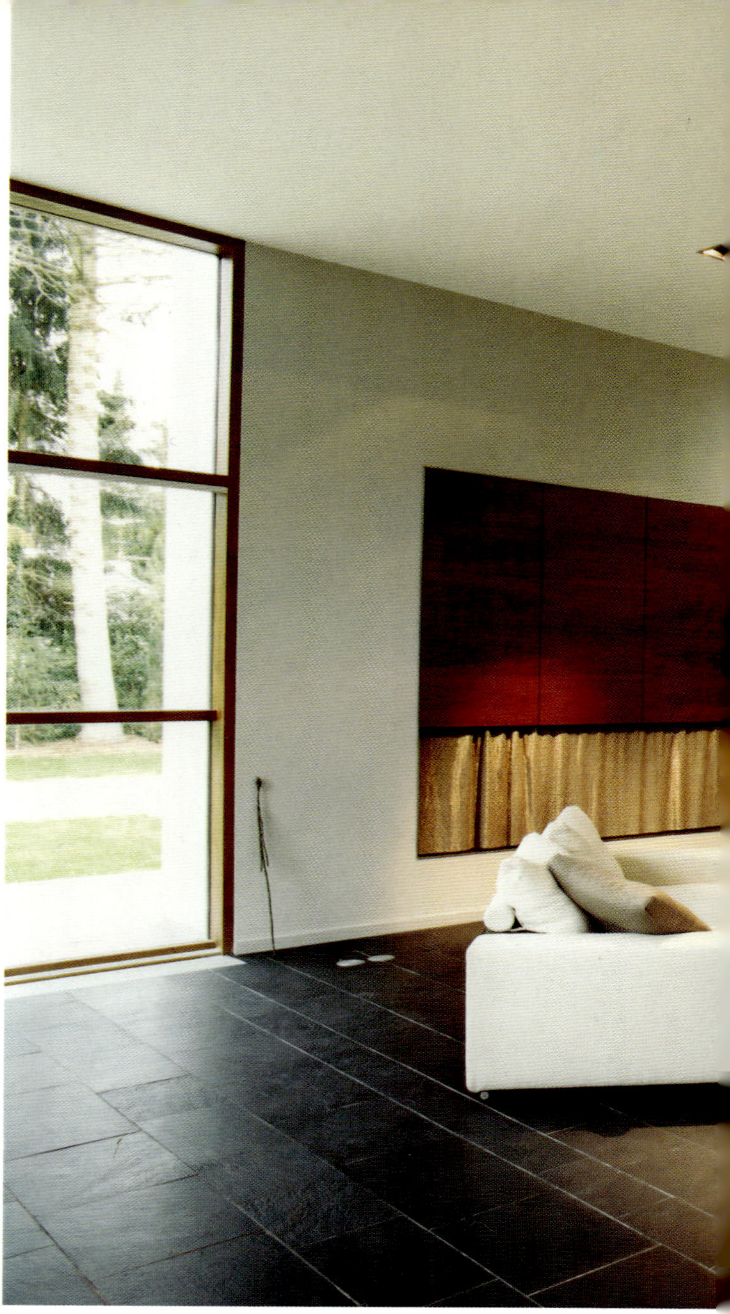

Combining **traditional structural forms** with a **modern spirit**

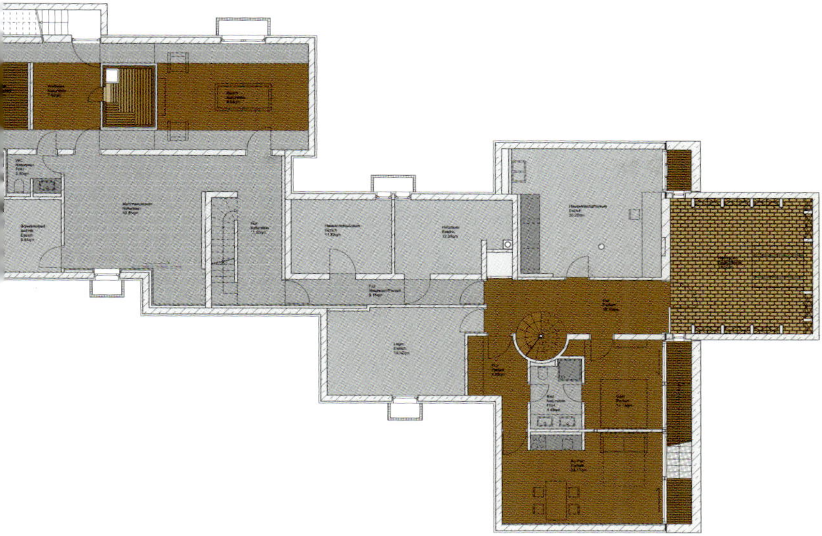

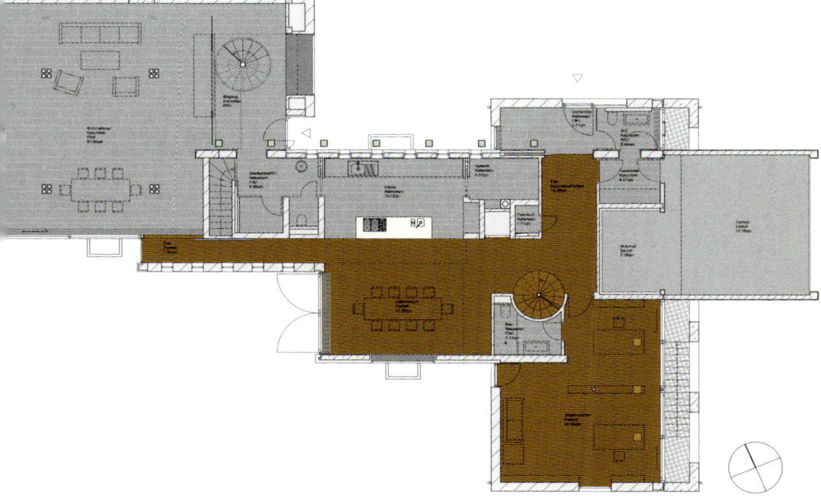

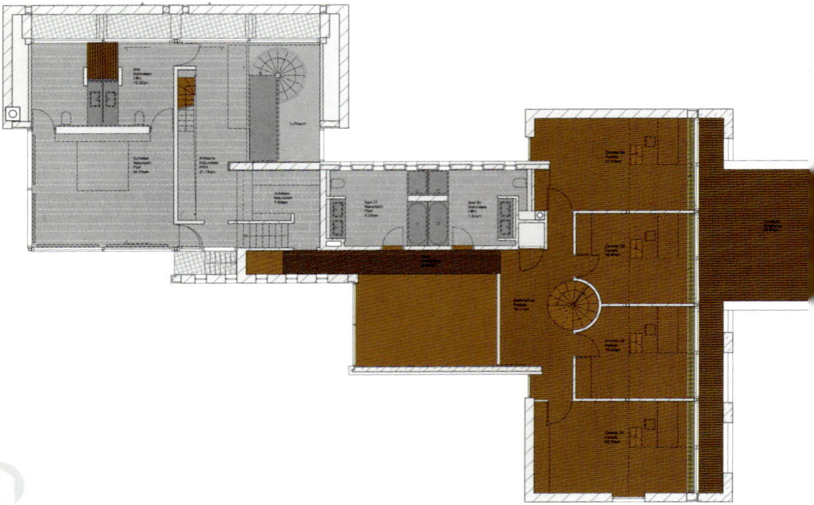

Living Box Wolken Küblis | Küblis | ARCHITEAM 4

Like a UFO made of wooden cubes, glass and concrete

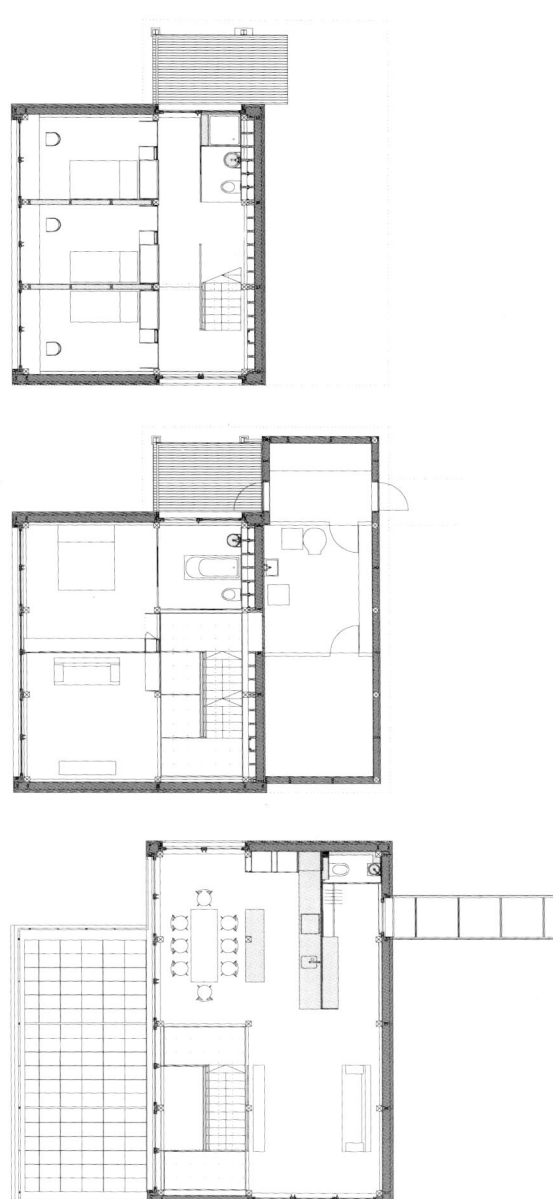

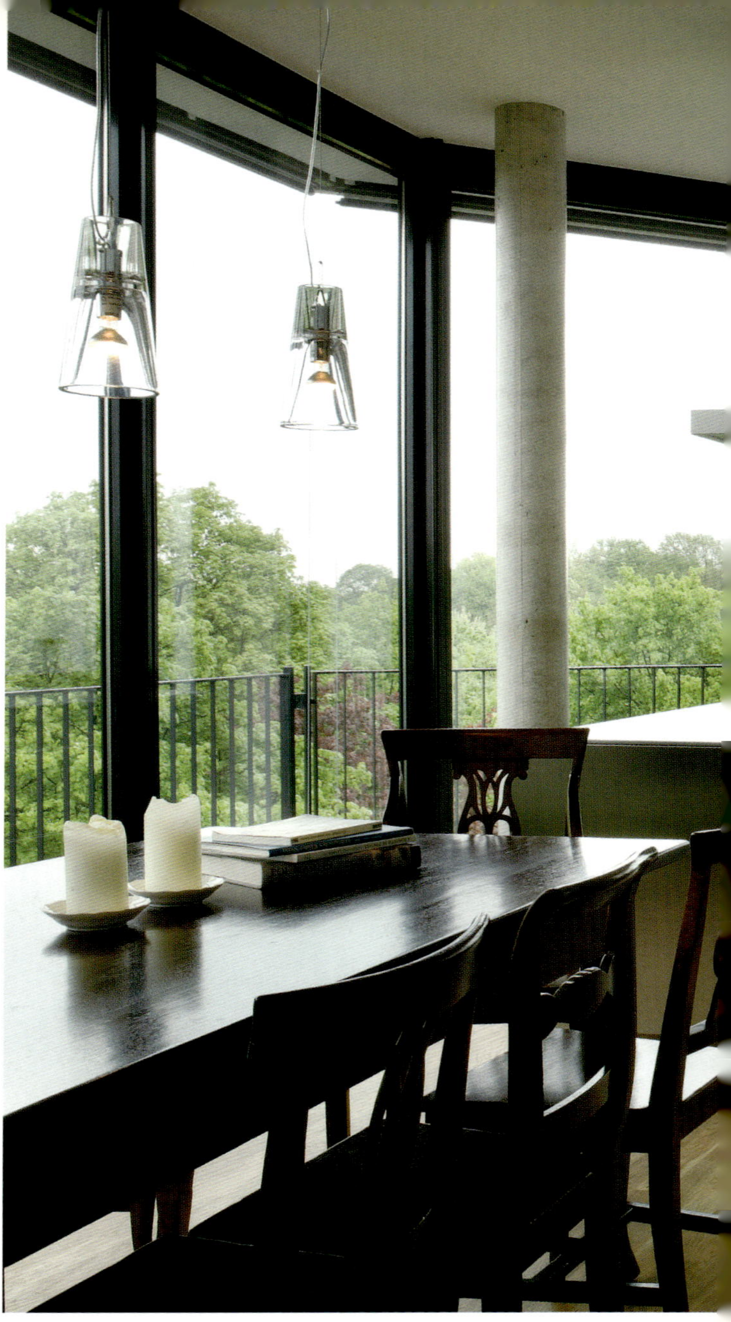

Transforming an **air-raid shelter** into a **modern house** with a **luxury loft**

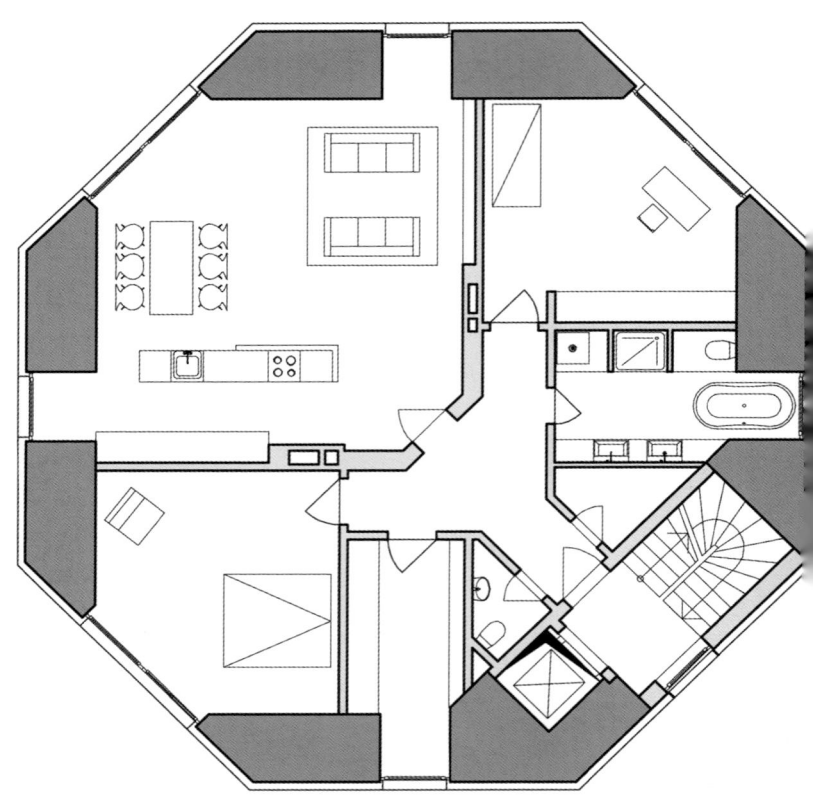

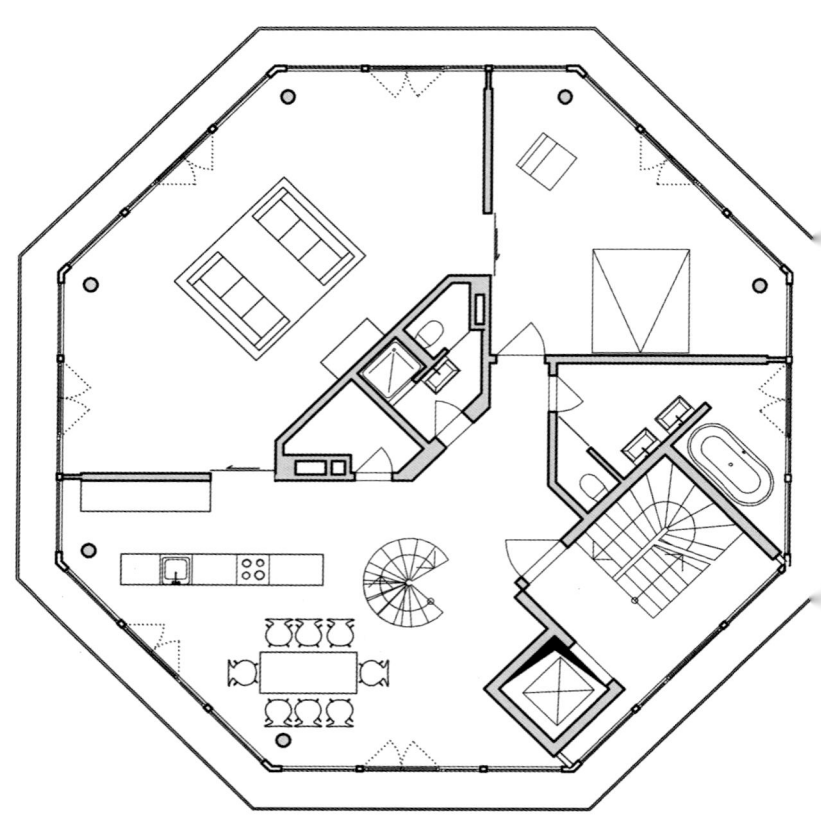

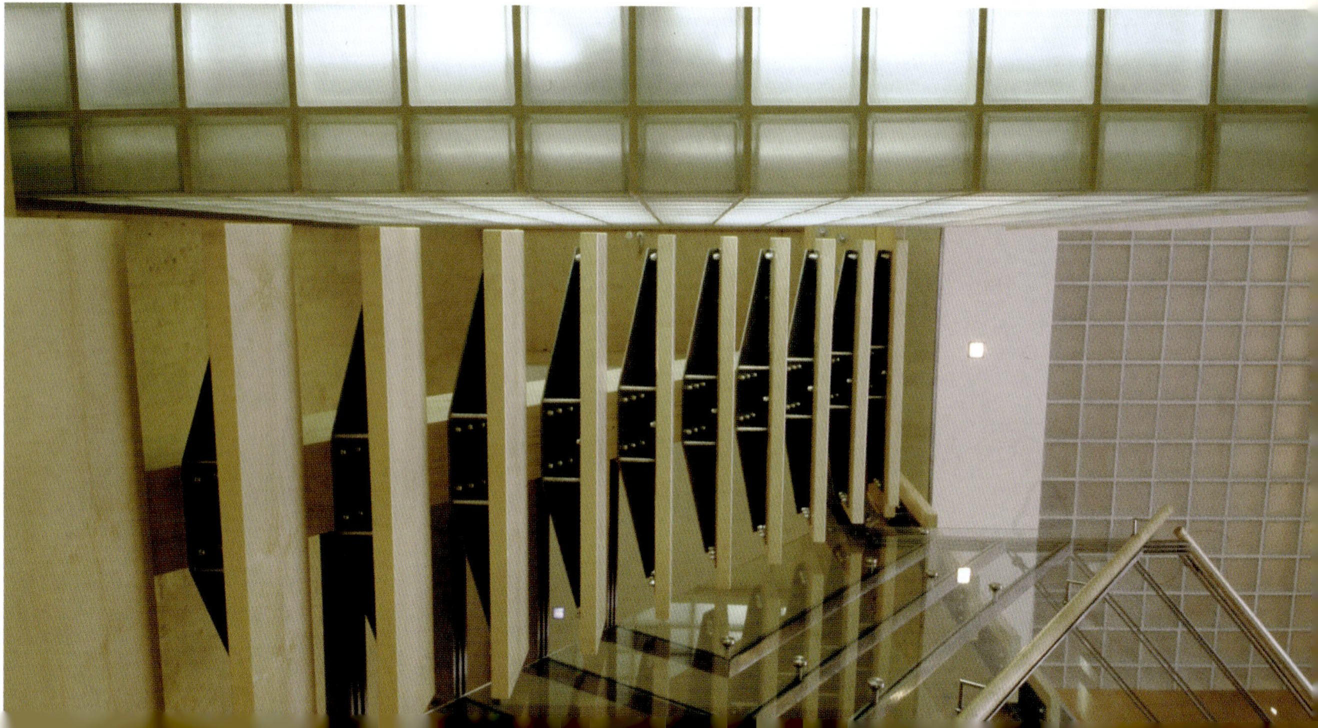

Original ideas combined **with comfort**

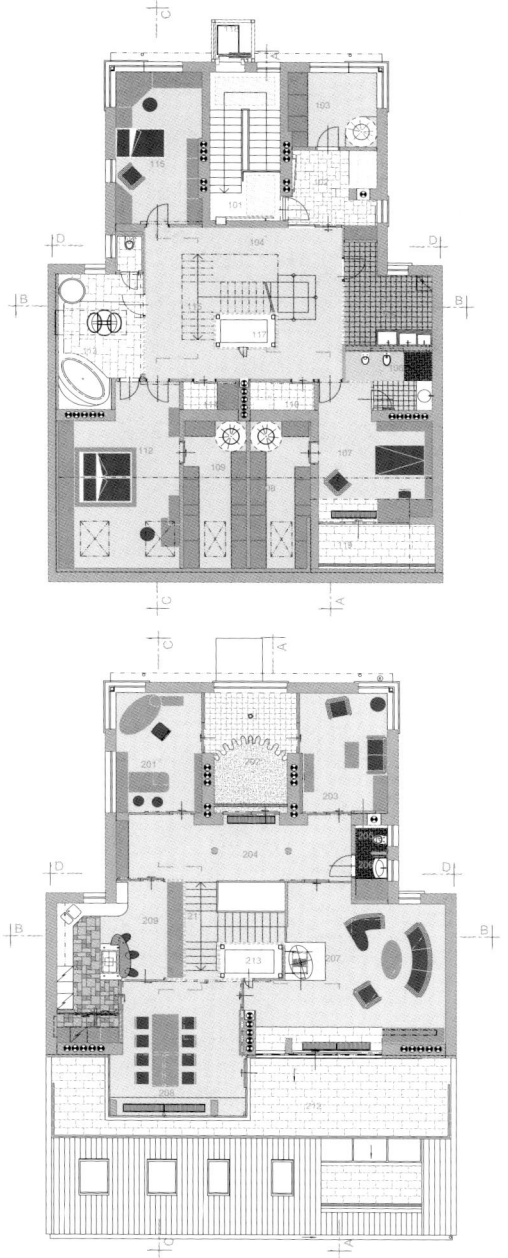

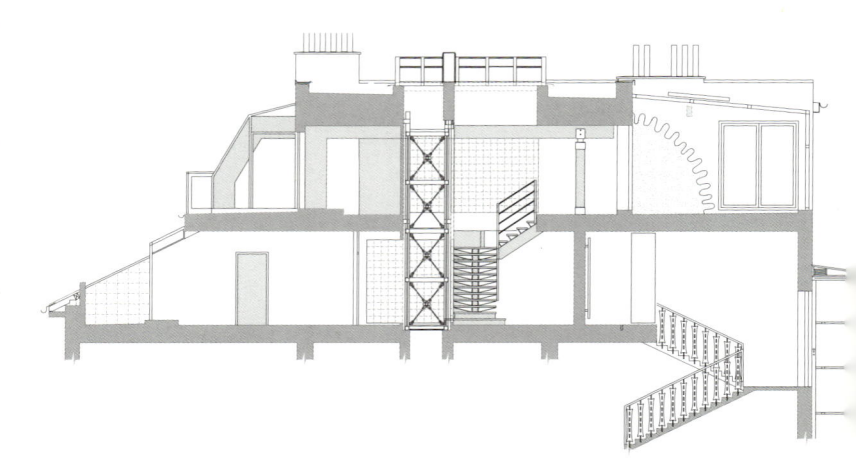

Ocean of Love | itinerant | Egg and Dart Design Cooperation

The design **follows an algorithm** of **external/ internal,** public/private **space**

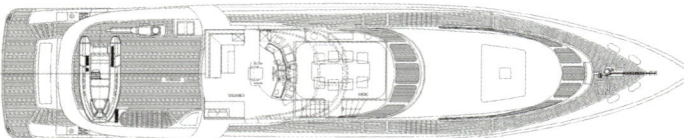

UPPER DECK

MAIN DECK

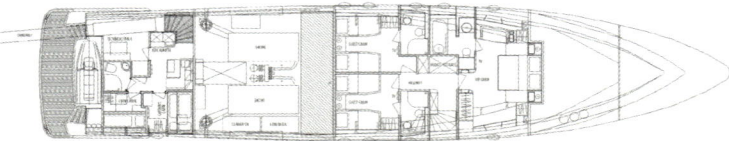

LOWER DECK

Scenic views and minimal design

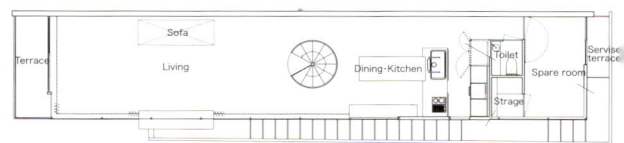

2nd Floor Plan

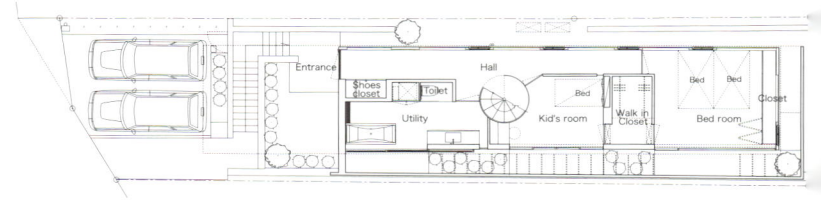

1st Floor Plan

| **Private Residence in Berlin** | Berlin | Dopo Domani

Playful decors and stylish furniture in historic shells

Meditative ambience
reminiscent of beach
and sea

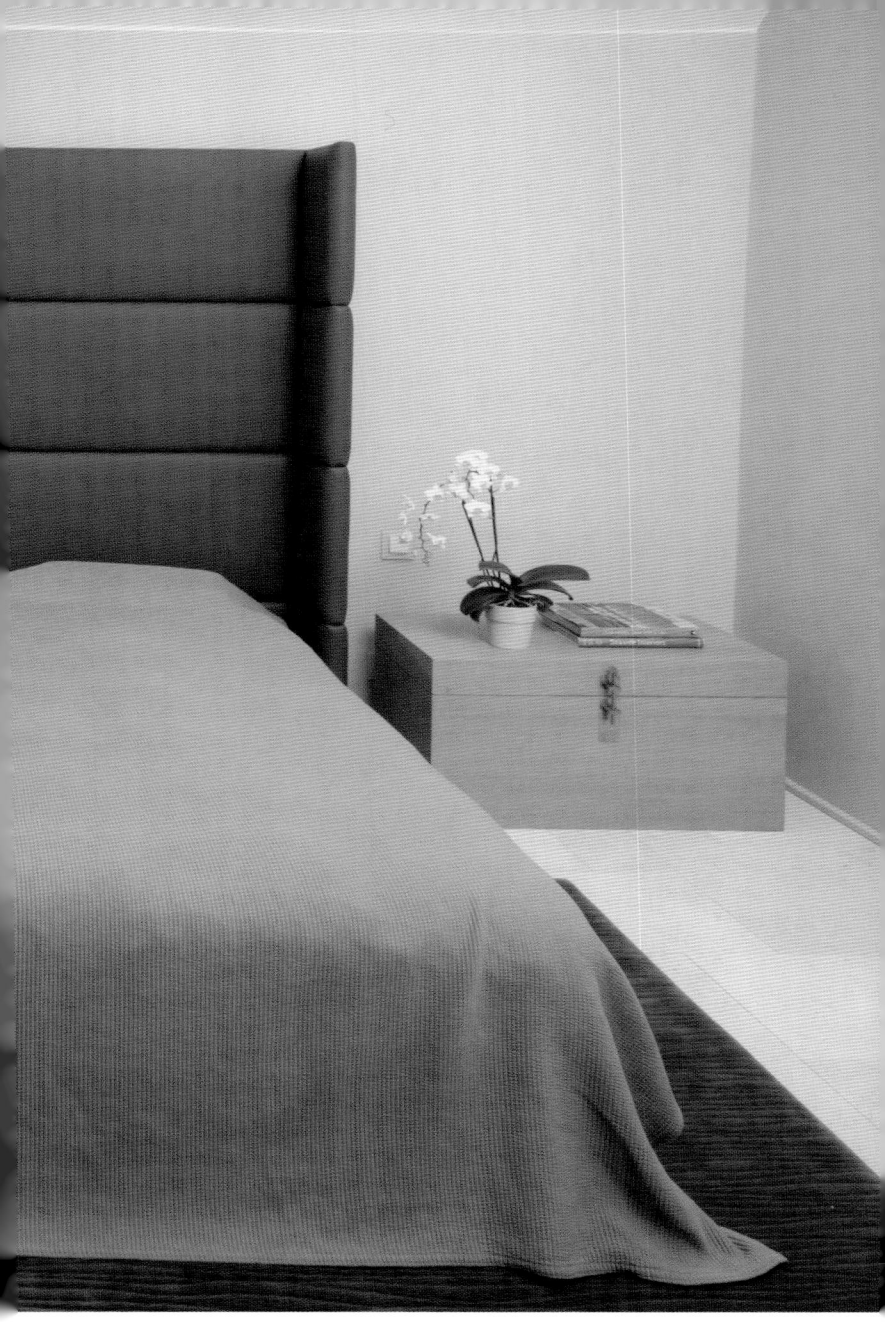

Redelco Residence | Studio City | Pugh + Scarpa Architects

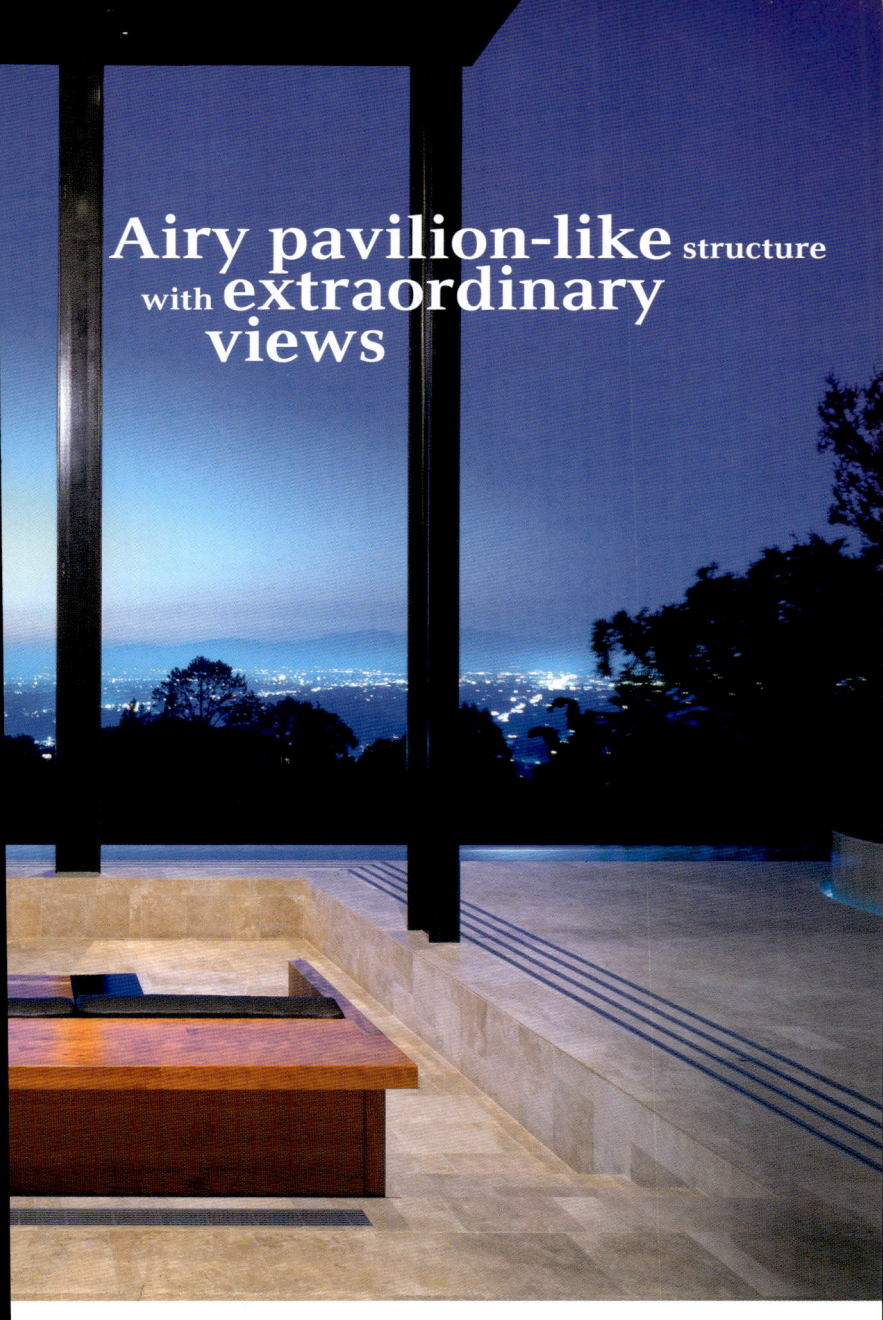

Airy pavilion-like structure with extraordinary views

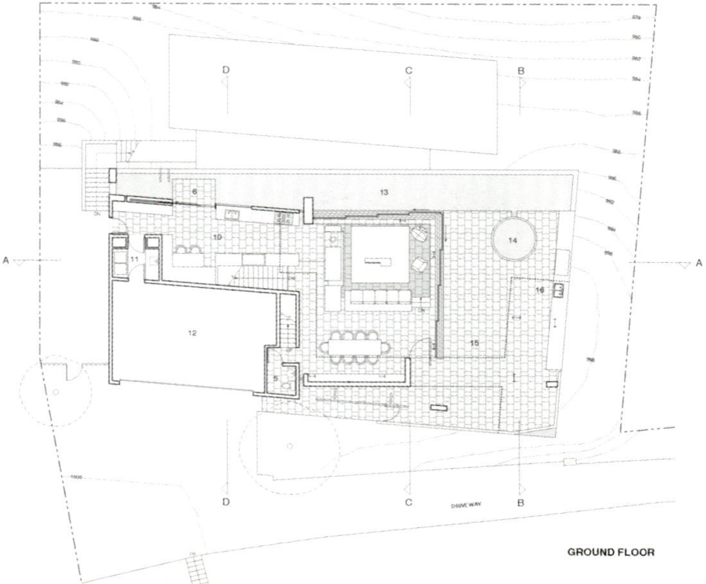

GROUND FLOOR

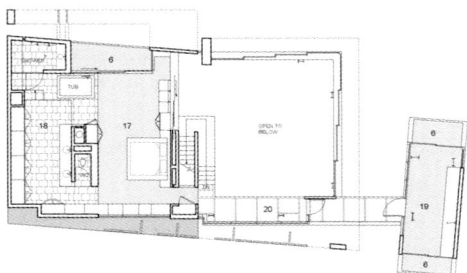

SECOND FLOOR

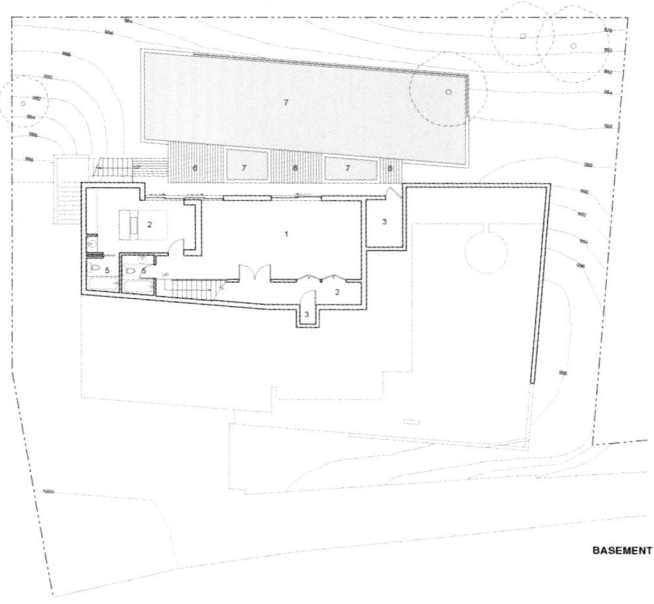

BASEMENT

Façade as filter to the city

Residential and office building in Alte Schönhauser Straße | Berlin | Angelis+Partner

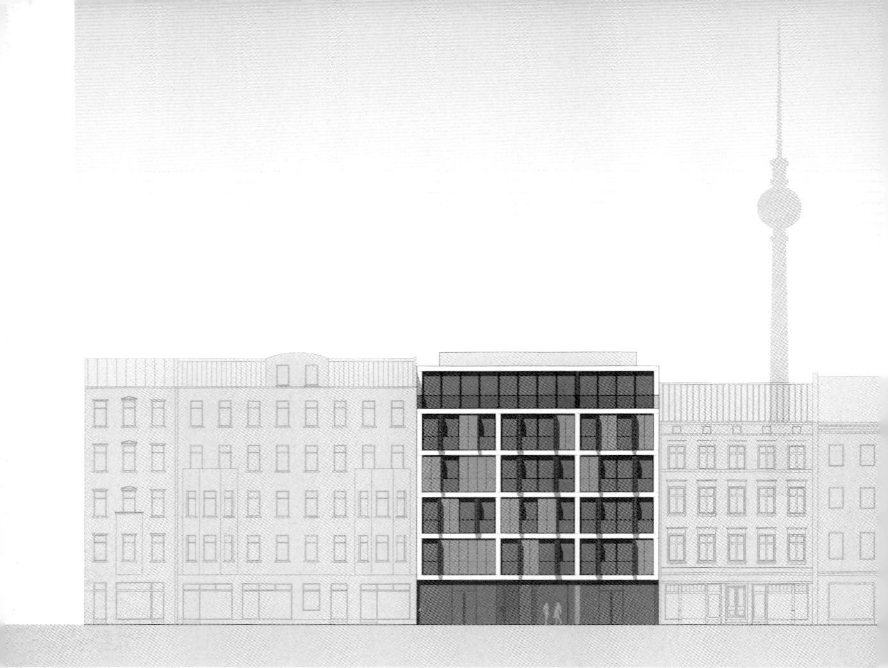

Schnitt B-B

Single Family House Im Lenz | Hinwil | Beat Rothen Architektur

Plain interior that concentrates on structures and materials

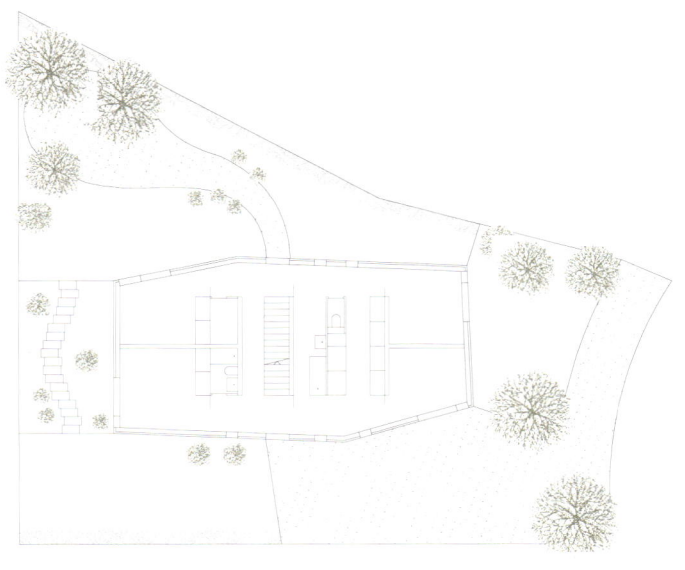

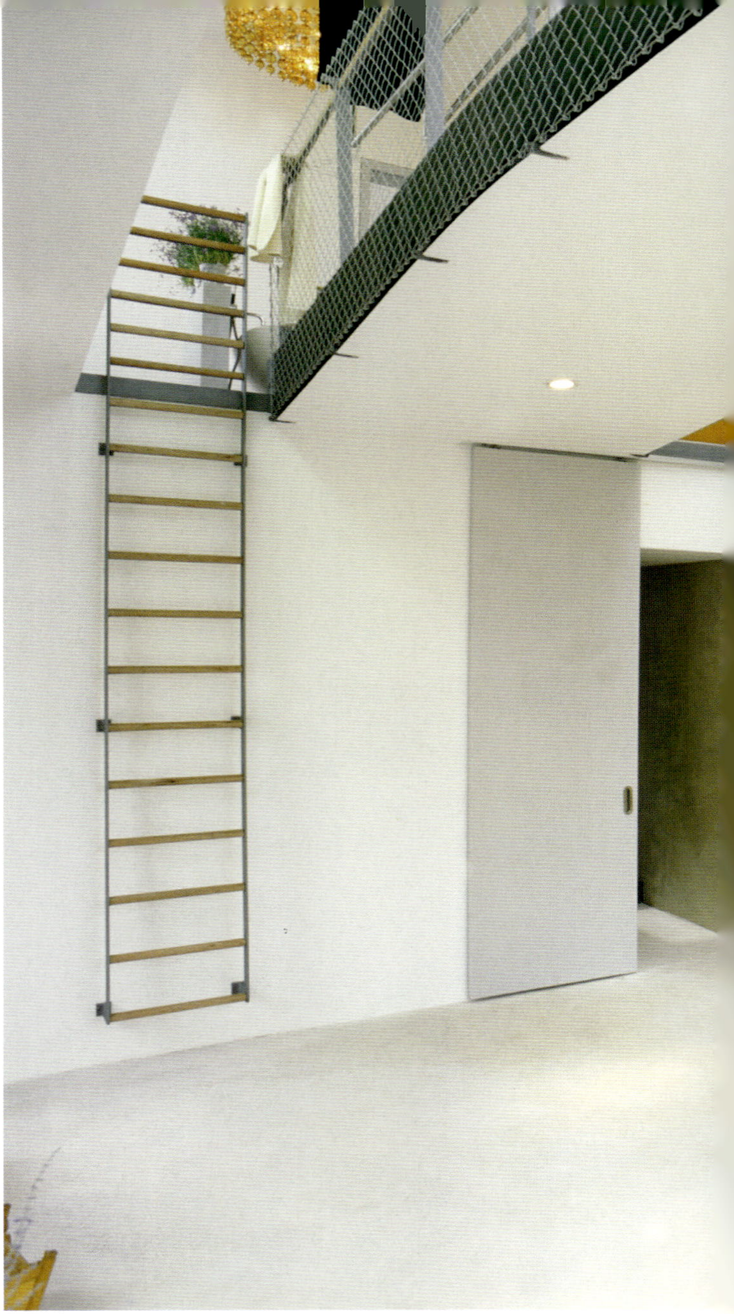

Looking to the future while incorporating the past

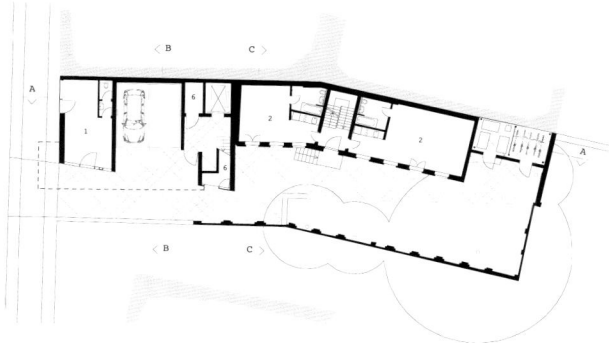

Bender: Ground floor

Legend: 1. Shop 2. Miniloft 3. Office 4. "House" 5. Roof terrace 6. Storage

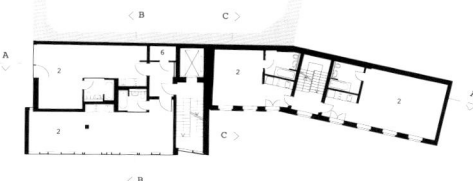

Bender: Typical floor

Legend: 1. Shop 2. Miniloft 3. Office 4. "House" 5. Roof terrace 6. Storage

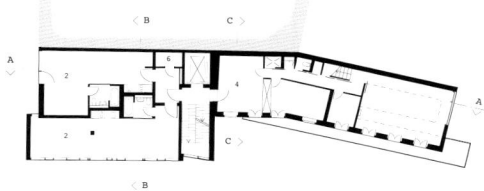

Bender: Third floor

Legend: 1. Shop 2. Miniloft 3. Office 4. "House" 5. Roof terrace 6. Storage

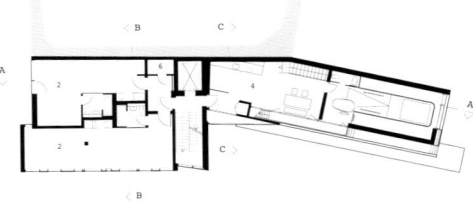

Bender: Fourth floor

Legend: 1. Shop 2. Miniloft 3. Office 4. "House" 5. Roof terrace 6. Storage

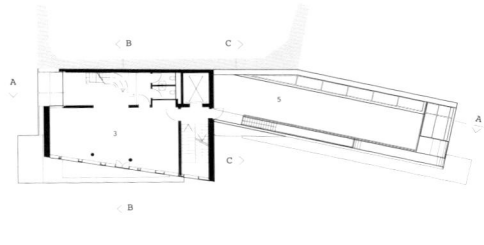

Bender: Fifth floor

Legend: 1. Shop 2. Miniloft 3. Office 4. "House" 5. Roof terrace 6. Storage

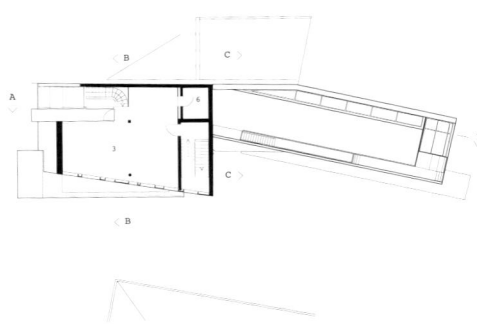

Bender: Sixth floor

Legend: 1. Shop 2. Miniloft 3. Office 4. "House" 5. Roof terrace 6. Storage

| **Space Winding** | Shanghai | MoHen Design International | Hank M. Chao

An **original** and **peaceful space** with **classical oriental** architecture

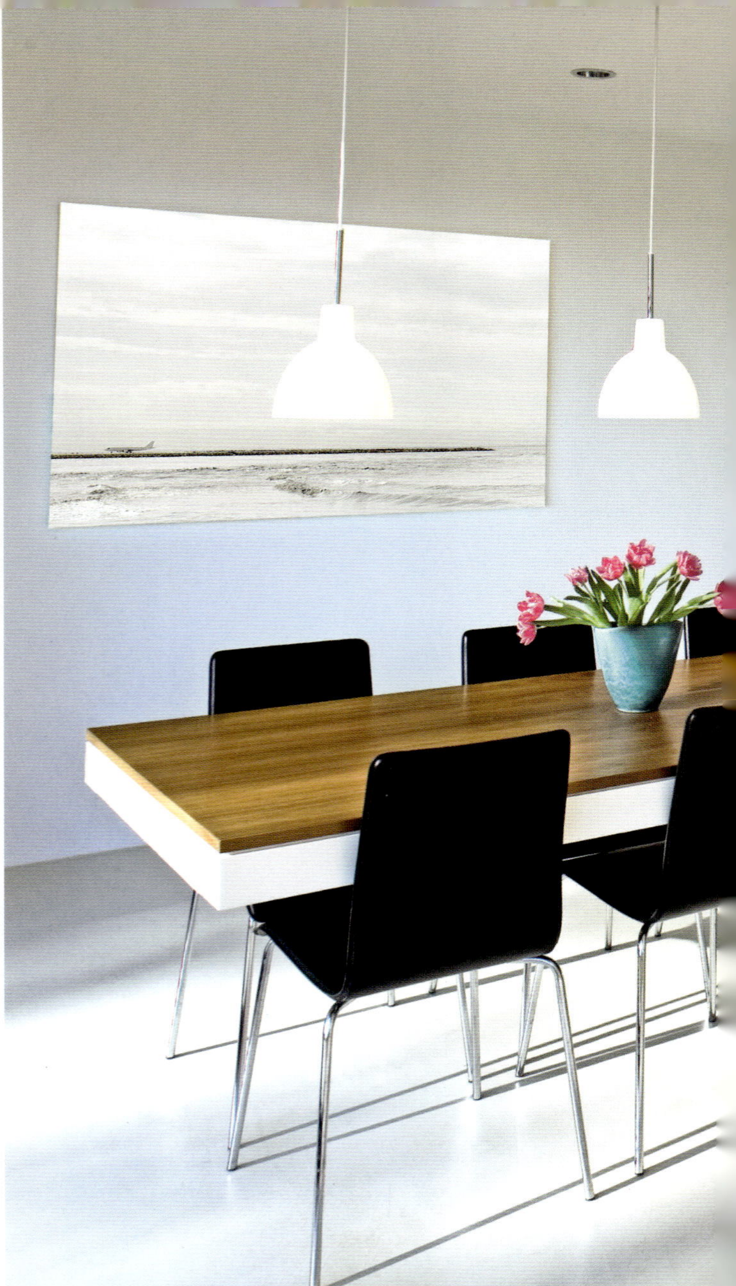

Monolithic sculptural T-shape that exudes **self-confidence**

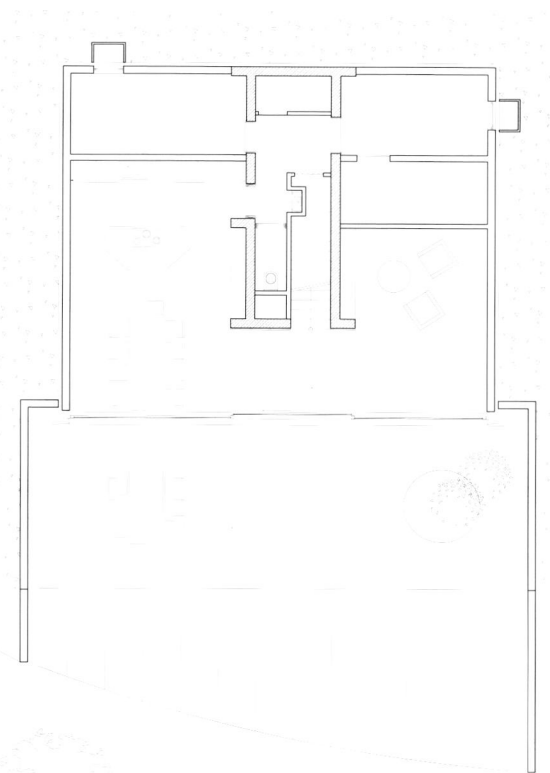

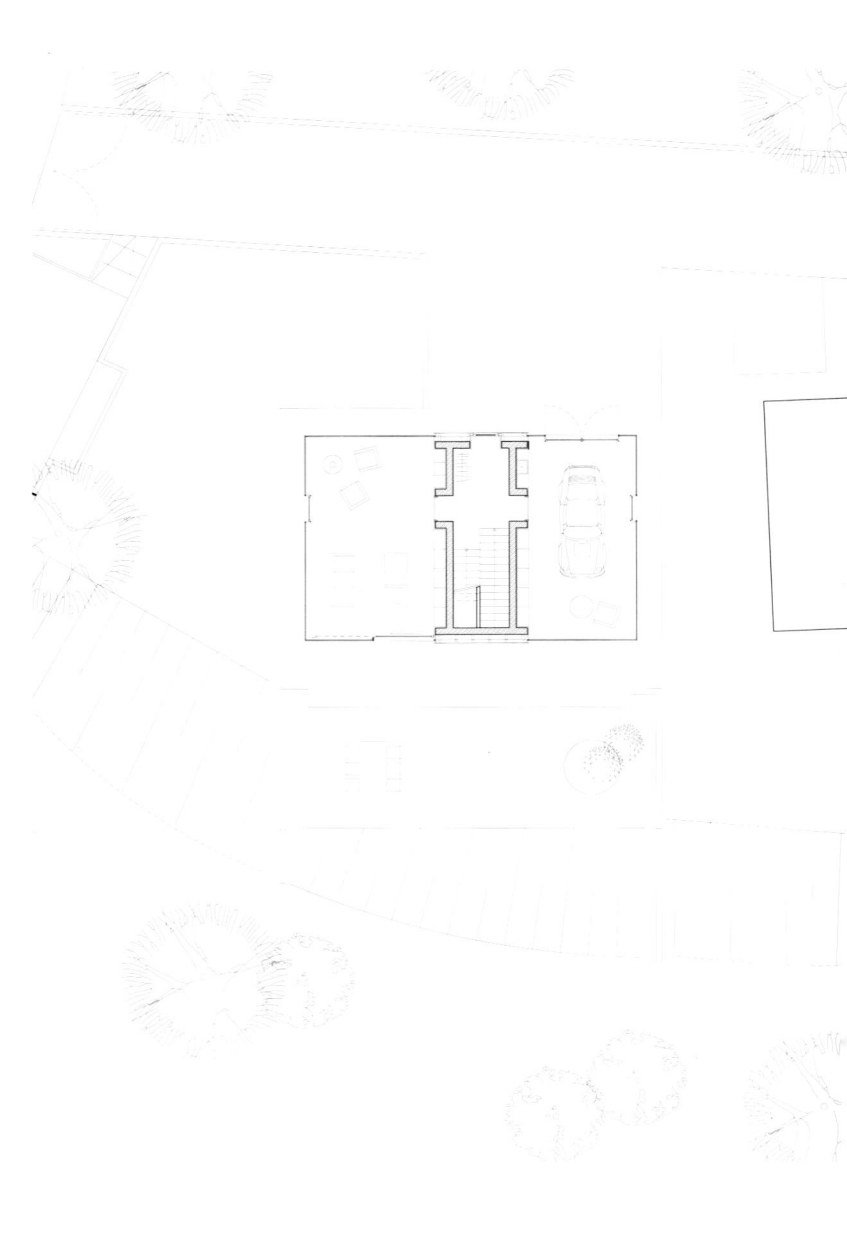

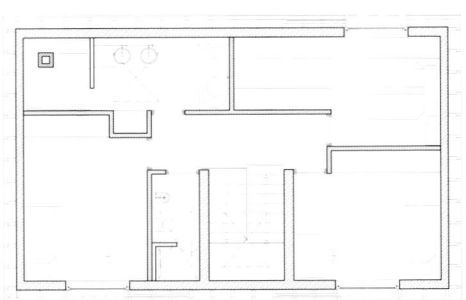

Matching colors
and **materials** create a
remarkable interior

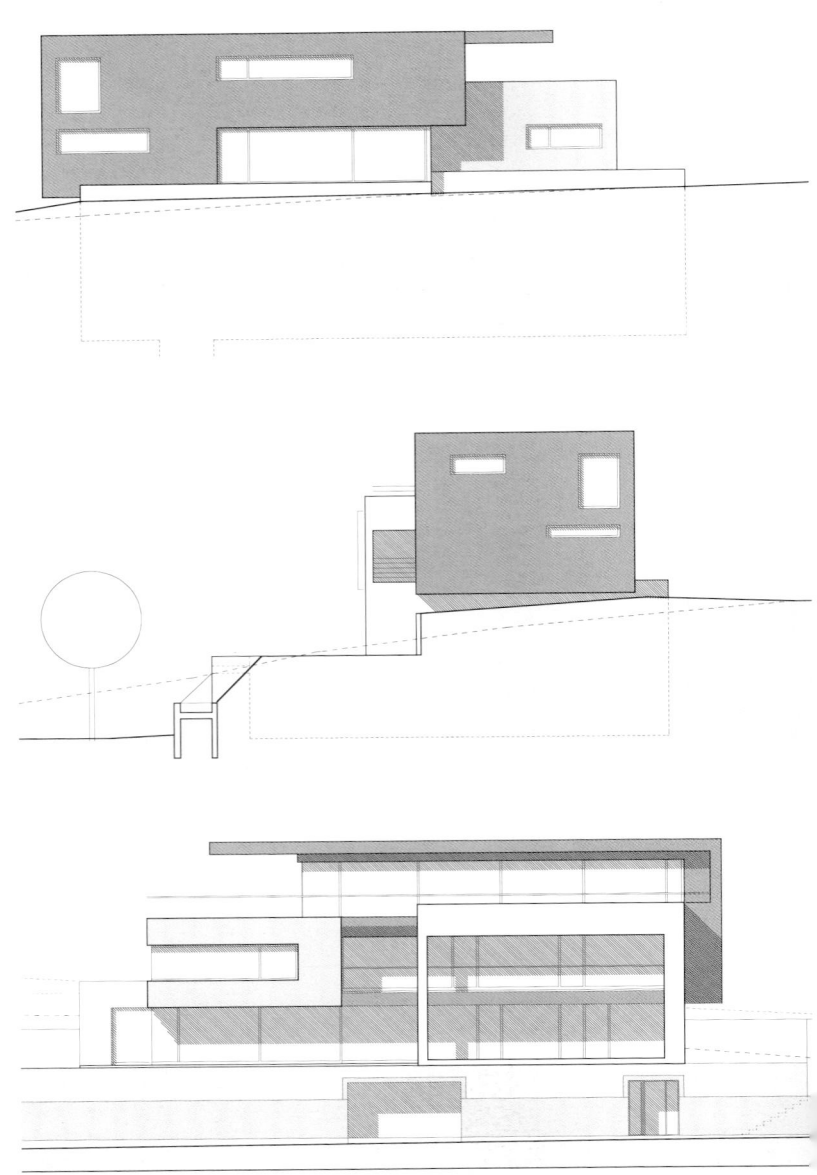

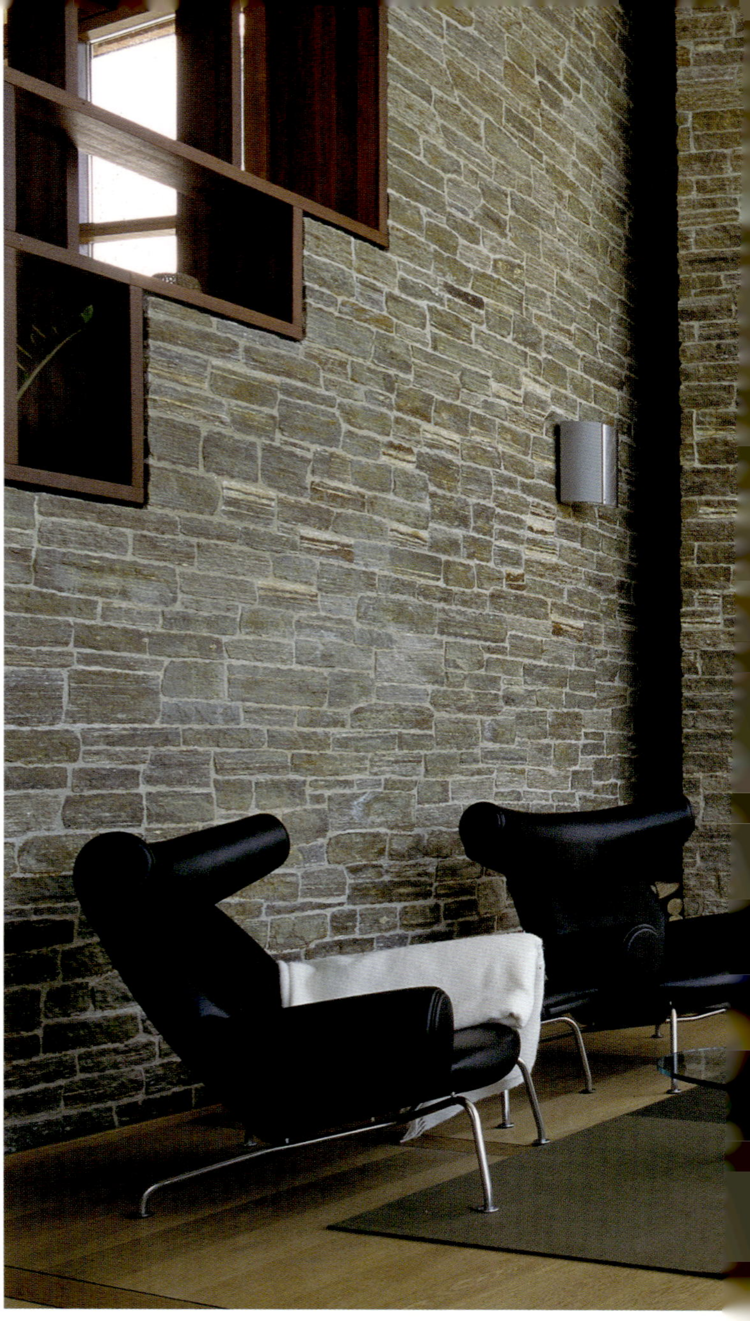

Symphony of materials and fireplace

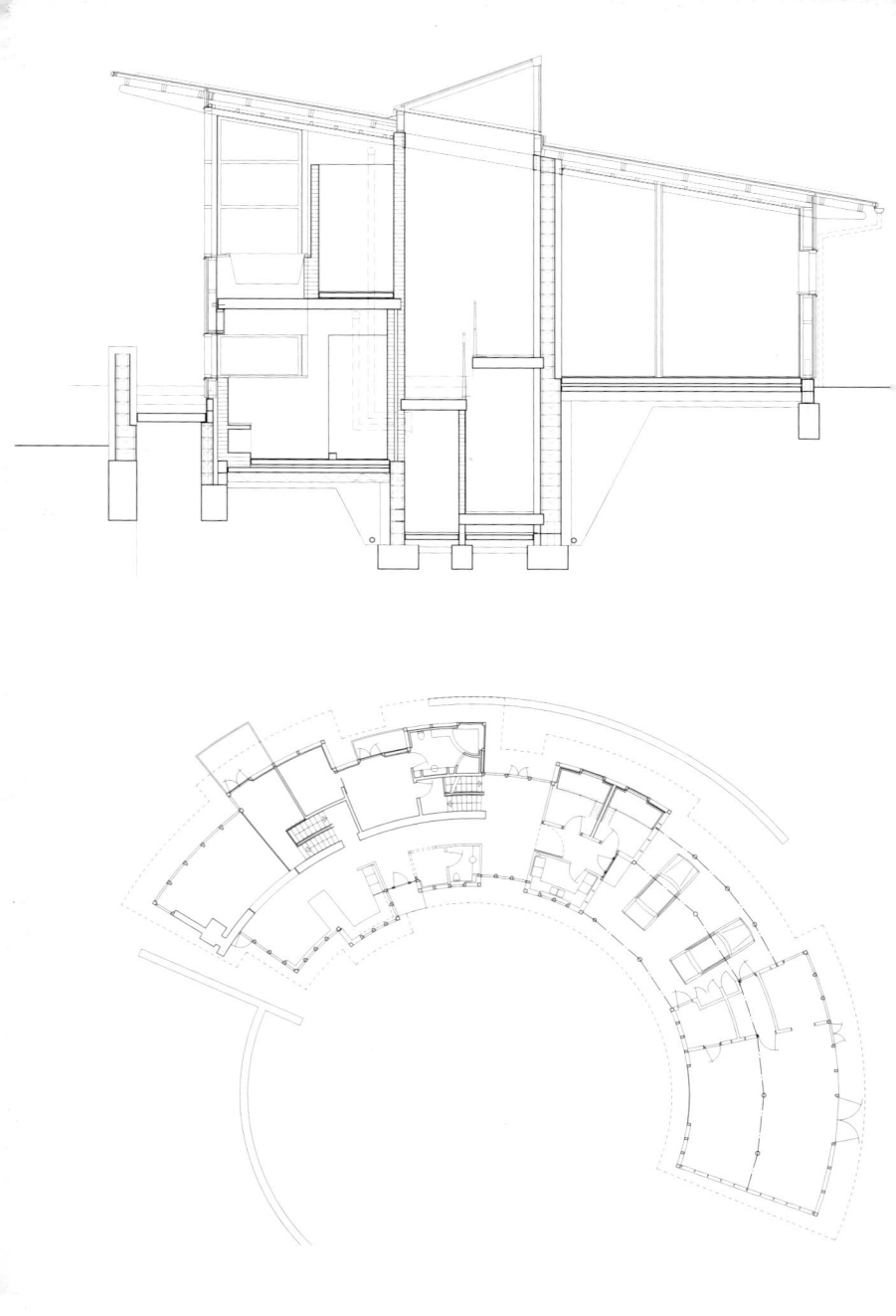

Seamless and wave-like arrangement on a sloping site

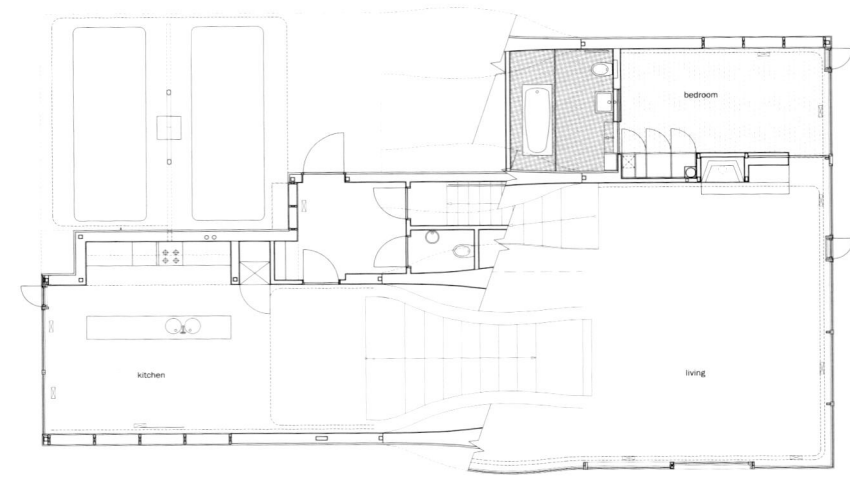

First Floor Plan

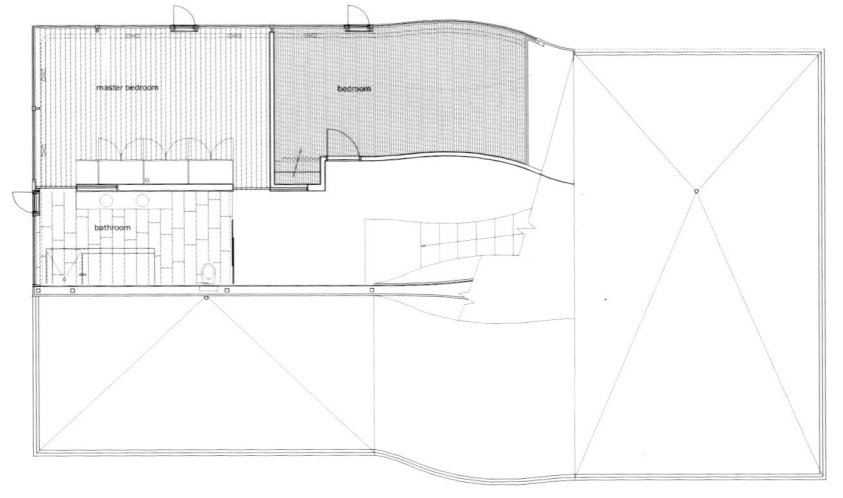

Second Floor Plan

VillAnn | Kungsbacka | Wingårdh Architektkontor

Rooms arranged along a line facing the sea

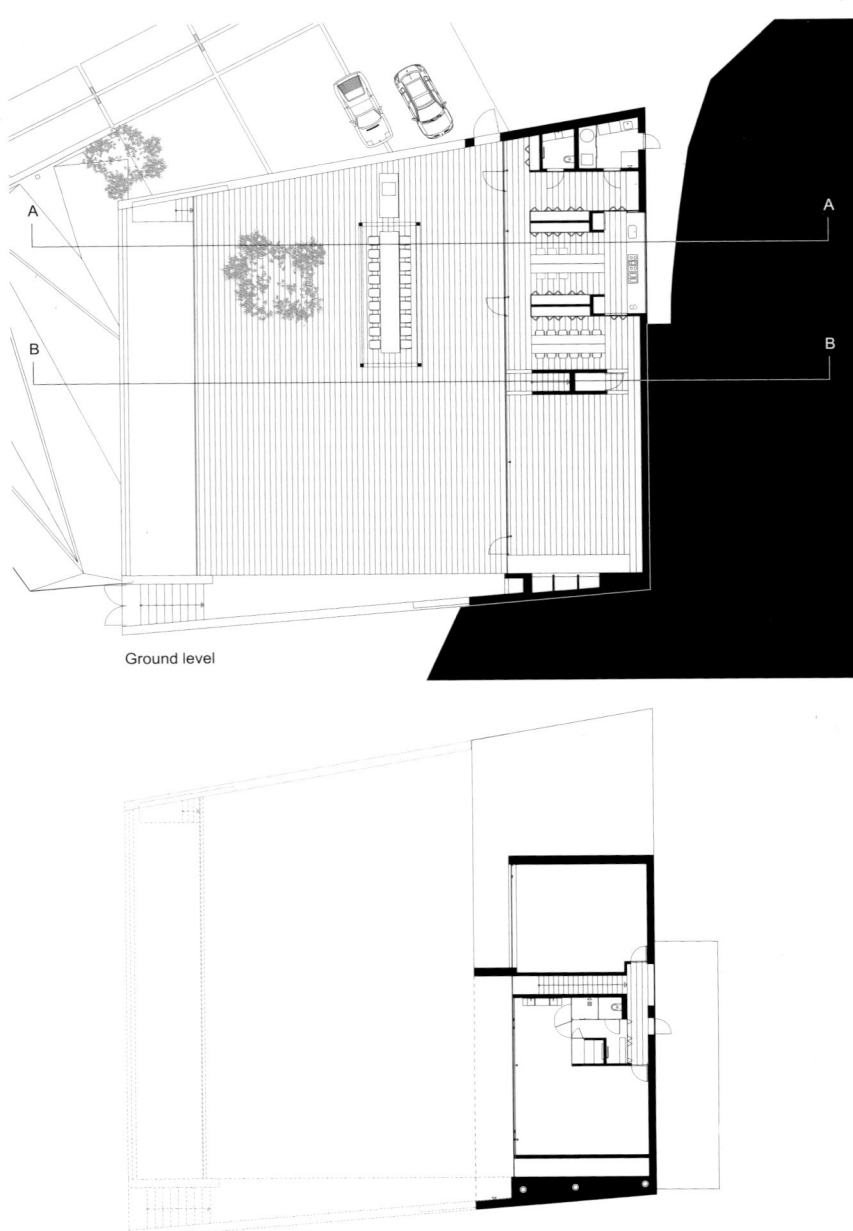

Ground level

Level 1

Natural colors, **crisp details** and **multiple textures** combined with **open spaces**

White Cave | Oita-shi Oita | TAKAO SHIOTUSKA ATELIER

Intersection between interior and exterior, based on white color and concrete

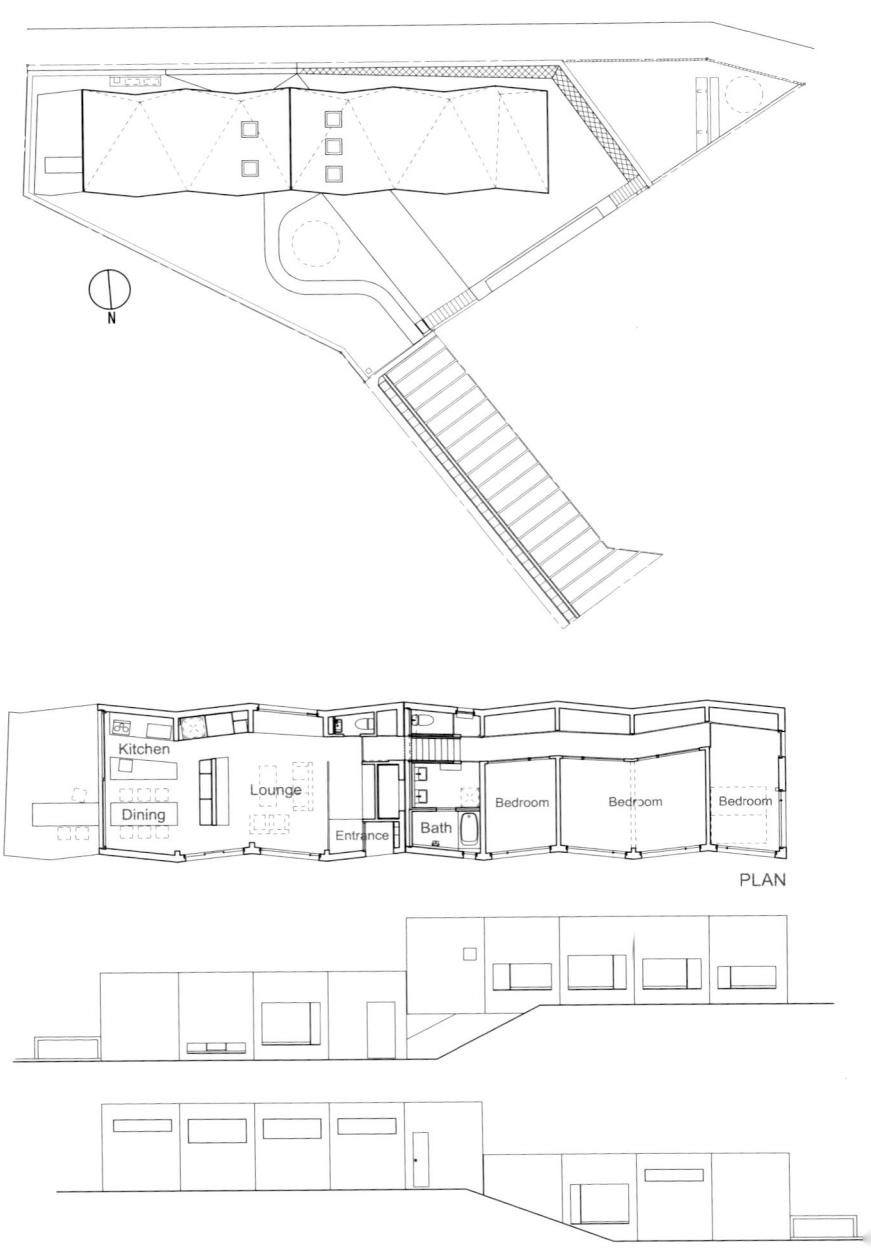

N

Kitchen

Lounge

Dining

Entrance

Bath

Bedroom

Bedroom

Bedroom

PLAN

Architects Index

Picture Credits